CONSTRUCTIVE CLINICAL SUPERVISION IN COUNSELING AND PSYCHOTHERAPY

Constructive Clinical Supervision in Counseling and Psychotherapy articulates a practical, theoretical approach to supervision that integrates salient elements of a number of diverse but complementary theoretical perspectives from the fields of human development, psychotherapy, and clinical supervision to assist in facilitating supervisee growth and change from a constructivist framework. This constructive approach to supervision is designed to serve as a practical, integrative meta-theory for supervisors of any theoretical orientation. For readers who already identify with constructivist ideas, this book will provide a theoretical grounding for their work, along with strategies to deepen their clinical practice. For those who are new to constructivist thinking, this book offers an innovative possibility for conceptualizing their role as clinical supervisors and alternative interventions to consider during times of impasse.

Douglas A. Guiffrida, PhD, is associate professor in the Margaret Warner Graduate School of Education and Human Development at the University of Rochester. He is an approved clinical supervisor, a nationally certified counselor, and a licensed mental health counselor in New York State.

CONSTRUCTIVE CLINICAL SUPERVISION IN COUNSELING AND PSYCHOTHERAPY

Douglas A. Guiffrida

Routledge
Taylor & Francis Group

NEW YORK AND LONDON

First published 2015
by Routledge
711 Third Avenue, New York, NY 10017

and by Routledge
27 Church Road, Hove, East Sussex BN3 2FA

Routledge is an imprint of the Taylor & Francis Group, an informa business

Library of Congress Cataloging-in-Publication Data
Guiffrida, Douglas A., author.
Constructive clinical supervision in counseling and psychotherapy / by
  Douglas A. Guiffrida.
    p. ; cm.
  Includes bibliographical references and index.
  I. Title.
  [DNLM: 1. Counseling—organization & administration.
2. Professional Competence—standards. 3. Psychological Theory.
4. Psychotherapy—organization & administration.   5. Staff Development.
WM 21]
BF637.C6
616.89'14—dc23   2014026973

ISBN: 978-0-415-70490-8 (hbk)
ISBN: 978-0-415-70491-5 (pbk)
ISBN: 978-1-315-89022-7 (ebk)

Typeset in Bembo
by Apex CoVantage, LLC

To Amy, Ellie, and Sam

CONTENTS

Foreword by Janine M. Bernard   *ix*
Preface   *xi*
Acknowledgments   *xvii*

1   A Brief Introduction to Constructivist Counseling,
    Development, and Learning   1

2   Influential Theories of Psychotherapy   21

3   The Process of Constructive Supervision   48

4   Reflective Activities   75

5   Assessment   99

6   Answers to Common Questions about Constructive
    Clinical Supervision   117

Appendix: Constructive Supervisee Assessment   139

Index   *141*

FOREWORD

I do not self-identify as a constructivist. More importantly, no one who knows me would describe me as such. So, why am I excited about this book? First and foremost, as Guiffrida explains in his Preface, the book is designed to be a useful resource not only to those who are more steeped in constructivist approaches to therapy and supervision, but also to people like me. Although there has been an occasional article that articulates a constructivist approach to supervision, the mental health professions have yet to have a resource that is theoretically grounded and practical, and that wrestles with sticky (and endemic) issues like assessment. With Guiffrida's *Constructive Clinical Supervision*, we now have such a resource. As such, Guiffrida is making an important contribution to the evolution of our understanding of clinical supervision.

Guiffrida has more than done his homework in preparing to write this text. As a result, the book demonstrates a deep understanding of the theories he is blending in his approach and practical application that has been tested in his own teaching and supervision. In Guiffrida's words:

> I did not learn about constructivism in the classroom . . . Rather, I discovered this orientation through careful observation and reflection of my own practice and the practice of others: the things that were effective in understanding and helping supervisees were continually consistent with constructivist ideas of growth and change and the things that seemed to get in the way of effective supervision were not.

In short, Guiffrida has walked the walk that he espouses in this text. Furthermore, the book is exceedingly accessible due to Guiffrida's clarity of expression and avoidance of professional jargon.

Too often, books with a singular purpose become insular and avoid reference to issues that might represent the Achilles heel of the approach being presented. Therefore, I was particularly pleased to see Guiffrida's chapter on assessment within constructive supervision, taking head-on an issue that many outside of constructivist circles have with an approach that can be construed as supervisee-centered to the detriment of gatekeeping. Guiffrida's description of principles of traditional assessment versus constructivist assessment is a distinction that will be exceedingly helpful to new supervisors. In fact, I look forward to discussions with my students around these principles as they attempt to grapple with the larger theme of supervisee evaluation. Guiffrida walks the reader through a process from understanding principles to giving difficult feedback. Furthermore, by virtue of the theoretical bias of the book, self-assessment is discussed in a more convincing fashion than is often the case in other supervision texts. As self-assessment is a (often understated) goal of all clinical supervision, the focus here should be recognized as adding to the book's value.

I found the last chapter of the book to be a total delight. Guiffrida knows his broader audience and the place of constructive supervision within the discourse of the discipline at large. He answers his critics in a way that will further the reader's understanding of what he has presented in the chapters that preceded this one. He also is able to communicate his profound respect for supervisees and for the process of supervision.

In conclusion, having read this book, I look forward to the discussions it will stimulate between me and my students the next time I teach supervision. As someone outside the constructivist mindset, I experience this book as both inviting and intriguing. I am confident that it will resonate with many supervisors-in-training as they attempt to find an approach that honors their personal principles. On their behalf and my own, I thank Douglas Guiffrida for giving us the benefit of his learning and his experience.

Janine M. Bernard
Professor, Syracuse University, and
co-author of *Fundamentals of Clinical Supervision*

PREFACE

Clinical supervision is central to the successful training and ongoing professional development of counselors and psychotherapists. The importance of clinical supervision is most evident by the fact that all major state licensing boards and accrediting bodies within the various psychotherapy professions, including counseling, psychology, social work, and marriage and family therapy, require that students receive clinical supervision as part of their clinical training. In highlighting the importance of supervision to the training of helping professionals, Bernard and Goodyear (2014) went as far as labeling clinical supervision "the signature pedagogy" (p. 2) of psychotherapy in the same way that the Socratic dialogue is considered the signature pedagogy of law school. Additionally, ongoing supervision is often required to maintain one's professional status in these fields and, thus, remains a central aspect of psychotherapy well beyond the initial graduate-level training.

Clinical supervision is commonly defined as:

> an intervention provided by a more senior member of a profession to a more junior colleague or colleagues who typically (but not always) are members of that same profession. This relationship is (a) evaluative and hierarchical, (b) extends over time, and (c) has the simultaneous purposes of enhancing the professional functioning of the more junior person(s); monitoring the quality of professional services offered to the clients that she, he, or they see; and serving as a gatekeeper for the particular profession the supervisee seeks to enter.
>
> (Bernard & Goodyear, 2014, p. 9)

While clinical supervision shares much in common with psychotherapy, it is clear from the above definition that it is a distinct activity from psychotherapy that requires its own distinct theories and techniques. The use of theory is especially important in understanding the dynamic and complex practice of clinical supervision, which requires supervisors to conceptualize the often confusing and conflicting thoughts, feelings, and behaviors of their supervisee and their supervisee's clients. To add to this, supervisors must also pay attention to the complex interpersonal dynamics between clients, supervisees, and themselves. The multifaceted nature of clinical supervision led Bernard and Goodyear to conclude, "It would be impossible for a supervisor to negotiate this complexity without the benefit of some theory" (p. 77).

In this book, I articulate a practical approach to supervision that integrates salient elements of a number of diverse, but complementary theoretical perspectives from the fields of human development, psychotherapy, and clinical supervision to assist in facilitating supervisee growth and change from a constructivist framework. I refer to this integrative approach as *Constructive Supervision*, which is a term I have borrowed from Michael Mahoney's (2006) seminal book titled, *Constructive Psychotherapy: Theory and Practice*. Like Mahoney, I have opted to use the word *constructive* to denote the positive and flexible nature of this approach to supervision rather than using the terms *constructivist* or *constructionist*, which some readers may associate with a strict set of rules based on philosophical underpinnings. Also consistent with Mahoney's constructive theory of psychotherapy, the constructive approach to supervision outlined in this book is designed to serve as a practical, integrative meta-theory for supervisors of any theoretical orientation who are seeking to add depth, breadth, and novelty to the practice of clinical supervision.

While Mahoney's *constructive* approach to psychotherapy forms the conceptual basis of the constructive approach to supervision outlined in this book, the current approach also deviates from Mahoney's approach to psychotherapy in several ways. Some of the deviations are necessary in translating the work from psychotherapy to supervision; while the two fields share considerable overlap, supervision is distinct in many ways from psychotherapy and these differences necessitate some alternative applications of the same constructivist principles. Other differences between this application of constructivist ideas to supervision and Mahoney's constructive psychotherapy derive from subtle differences in our interpretations and approaches to helping. Therefore, while I believe the approach outlined in this book is firmly rooted in Mahoney's constructive theory of psychotherapy, it is, nonetheless, a slightly alternative interpretation that is applied to a different population (supervisees rather than clients).

In addition to drawing heavily from Mahoney's constructive approach to psychotherapy, I have also relied extensively on the work of several other contemporary constructivist authors in developing this approach to supervision, including those who have developed constructivist approaches to conceptualizing human development, conducting psychotherapy, and providing psychotherapy training. Although the constructive approach outlined in this book is grounded in previously developed research and theory, the central ideas have also been developed through my work as a supervisor, as an instructor of a doctoral-level clinical supervision course, and as a supervisor of supervisors. In addition to critically reflecting on my own experiences as a supervisor, I have been fortunate to witness numerous supervision sessions with the supervisors who conducted the sessions and to help these supervisors process, understand, and improve upon these complex experiences.

I did not learn about constructivism in the classroom before applying the ideas to supervision. Rather, I discovered this orientation through careful observation and reflection of my own practice and the practice of others: the things that were effective in understanding and helping supervisees were continually consistent with constructivist ideas of growth and change and the things that seemed to get in the way of effective supervision were not. Ultimately, it was this collaborative process of helping supervisors deconstruct and re-construct their supervision sessions, continually reflecting on my own practice, and searching for literature that helped explain what was happening that allowed me to understand the supervisory process in the ways outlined in this book.

It is important to note several assumptions that are inherent in the book. The first is that, as pointed out by Bernard and Goodyear (2014), mental health professions, including counseling, psychology, marriage and family therapy, and social work are "more alike than different in their approach to supervision" (p. 3). While I use the words "counselor" or "psychotherapist" throughout the book, the ideas are relevant to and written for supervisors from any of the aforementioned helping professions. Second, the book is written specifically for practitioners who are learning or currently practicing supervision. As a result, I present only a cursory review of the various theories associated with the approach and have kept theoretical jargon to a minimum to focus on the applied aspects of supervision. Readers are encouraged to refer to Mahoney (2006) and Neimeyer and Mahoney (1995) for more detailed historical discussions and theoretical descriptions of constructivism and constructivist psychotherapy. Third, because the book is written for practicing psychotherapists, I assume readers will have a fundamental knowledge of basic counseling terminology, theories, and influential theorists; therefore, I do not provide extensive discussions or details about these elementary aspects of the profession.

It is also important to note that this book, unlike most other clinical supervision books that I have reviewed, does not provide a comprehensive review of the entire landscape of clinical supervision research, theory, and practice; rather, this book is intended to outline one particular theoretical approach to supervision, in the same way that a book articulating a theory of counseling would not attempt to describe all aspects of the field of counseling. Readers are encouraged to review a clinical supervision textbook, such as Bernard and Goodyear's (2014) *Fundamentals of Clinical Supervision,* for a more comprehensive review of the field of clinical supervision and detailed descriptions of salient issues that are not directly addressed in this book.

I begin in Chapter 1 by briefly describing constructivism, including constructivist views of development and human change processes. Included are overviews of the Developmental-Constructivist Theory of Human Change Processes (Mahoney, 2006), theories of counselor and counselor trainee development (McAuliffe & Eriksen, 2011; Skovholt & Ronnestad, 1992; Stoltenberg & McNeil, 2010), and a constructivist approach to counselor education (Guiffrida, 2005). Within each section are brief descriptions of how these constructivist ideas of growth, change, and learning can be used by supervisors to understand the complex experiences of their supervisees, normalize rather than pathologize difficult aspects of changes for supervisees, and develop interventions based on their supervisees' unique developmental needs.

In Chapter 2, I outline the theories of psychotherapy that are most salient when implementing a constructive approach to supervision. While these theories are generally not considered *constructivist* theories of counseling when considered in isolation, I will demonstrate how they can be integrated to provide supervisors with the necessary tools to facilitate change in supervisees from a constructive perspective. The chapter begins with a description of the person-centered approach (Rogers, 1957), focusing specifically on the need to establish a close, empathic relationship between supervisors and supervisees; and on the benefits of facilitating a non-directive approach during supervision. Next I review Self-Determination Theory (SDT; Deci & Ryan, 1991), a theory of motivation that has recently been applied in counseling settings, and describe how the fundamental tenets of SDT can be applied by supervisors to foster intrinsic motivation in supervisees. Third, I review mindfulness (Kabat-Zinn, 1994) and Mindfulness-Based Therapy (e.g., Segal, Williams, & Teasdale, 2002) and detail how the core principles of mindfulness can be integrated into the practice of supervision to help establish strong supervisor/supervisee relationships, to assist supervisees in embracing new and unknown situations, and to reduce power differentials and supervisee fear of judgment and evaluation. I conclude this chapter by describing how supervisee defense mechanisms (Freud, 1949) can manifest during supervision as a means of resisting change and how supervisors can effectively work with (rather than battle) these defenses to facilitate growth and change in supervisees.

Whereas Chapters 1 and 2 provide the theoretical basis for the constructive approach to supervision, Chapter 3 provides a much more applied outline of the process of constructive supervision. I begin describing the process of constructive supervision by detailing the role that constructive supervisors take using Bernard's (1979) Discrimination Model as a guiding framework. Specifically, I describe the centrality of the consultant role to constructive supervision, while also including suggestions on when and how to deviate to more active teaching and counseling roles when necessary. Next, I describe the formats that are most conducive to facilitating supervisee development utilizing the constructive approach, which includes detailing how video and audiotape review can be used to effectively facilitate supervisee learning and reflection. I conclude the chapter by describing the ways in which constructive supervisors integrate theory into their work with supervisees by delineating an approach based on the *Emergence Model* of teaching counseling theory.

In Chapter 4 I offer a number of activities that supervisors can use to facilitate supervisee self-reflection during times when supervisees experience difficulty in developing their own answers. Each activity provides potential for supervisees to discover their own answers using a different medium, which range from various forms of artistic and written expression, to mindful attentiveness. These activities include metaphoric drawing activities, reflective writing exercises, metaphoric representation using the sand tray, and mindfulness-based activities. I also provide guidelines for introducing the activities, adapting the activities for use in both individual and small group supervision, and for conducting the activities in ways that are consistent with constructivist principles of learning, growth, and development.

In Chapter 5, I outline the process of supervisee assessment from a constructive perspective, which can be one of the most difficult aspects of clinical supervision. I begin by providing an overview of constructivist principles of assessment, which are drawn largely from constructivist psychotherapy literature. In doing so, I delineate key differences between constructivist principles of assessment and those used in traditional, behaviorist approaches to assessment. Next, I describe how constructivist principles of assessment can be integrated into the practice of clinical supervision from a constructive approach, focusing specifically on how supervisors can integrate self-assessment procedures into the assessment process. I also discuss how these constructivist principles of assessment can be used in conjunction with more traditional forms of assessment. Additionally, I outline an instrument that can be used to assess supervisee growth and development specifically from a constructive perspective. I conclude this chapter by providing suggestions on how to present difficult feedback to supervisees who require additional learning experiences to attain proficiency in required competencies.

In the final chapter, I provide answers to a number of questions about the theory that have been asked by students during clinical supervision classes, colleagues during professional presentations and discussions, and reviewers and editors of this book. Topics range from how to ethically manage gatekeeping responsibilities, how to work with supervisees who struggle in developing their own answers, to the experiences that led me to consider supervision in this way. These questions have been invaluable in assisting me in thinking more deeply about the approach; it is my hope that my answers to them will provide readers with additional clarity regarding the more applied aspects of the approach and the rationale behind these applications.

For readers who already identify with postmodern approaches to supervision, my intention is to provide a resource to help you deepen your existing clinical practice. For others who are more familiar with and accustomed to modernist or behaviorist approaches to supervision, this proposed theory offers a new possibility for conceptualizing your role as a clinical supervisor and alternative interventions to consider during times of impasse. The book, however, represents merely one way of interpreting and applying constructivist ideas to the practice of supervision among many possibilities. Much work remains to help supervisors more fully comprehend and harness the potential of constructivist ideas to the practice of clinical supervision.

For information about earning continuing education credit for the learning associated with reading this book, go to www.warner.rochester.edu/researchprojects/projects/supervision.

References

Bernard, J.M. (1979). Supervisor training: A discrimination model. *Counselor Education and Supervision, 19*, 60–68.

Bernard, J.M., & Goodyear, R.K. (2014). *Fundamentals of clinical supervision*. Boston: Merrill.

Deci, E.L., & Ryan, R.M. (1991). A motivational approach to self: Integration in personality. In R. Dienstbier (Ed.), *Nebraska Symposium on Motivation: Vol. 38. Perspectives on motivation* (pp. 237–288). Lincoln, NE: University of Nebraska Press.

Freud, S. (1949). *An outline of psychoanalysis* (J. Strachey, trans.). New York: Norton.

Guiffrida, D.A. (2005). The emergence model: An alternative pedagogy for facilitating self-reflection and theoretical fit in counseling students. *Counselor Education and Supervision, 44*, 201–213.

Kabat-Zinn, J. (1994). *Wherever you go there you are: Mindfulness meditation in everyday life.* New York: Hyperion.

Mahoney, M.J. (2006). *Constructive psychotherapy: Theory and practice.* New York: Guilford

McAuliffe, G.J., & Eriksen, K.P. (2011). *Handbook of counselor preparation: Constructivist, developmental, and experiential approaches.* Thousand Oaks, CA: Sage.

Neimeyer, R.A., & Mahoney, M.J. (1995). *Constructivism in psychotherapy.* Washington, DC: American Psychological Association.

Rogers, C.R. (1951). *Client-centered therapy: Its current practice, implications and theory.* Boston, MA: Houghton Mifflin.

Rogers, C.R. (1957). The necessary and sufficient conditions of therapeutic personality change. *Journal of Consulting Psychology, 21*, 95–103.

Segal, Z.V., Williams, J.M.G., & Teasdale, J.D. (2002). *Mindfulness-based cognitive therapy for depression: A new approach to preventing relapse.* New York: Guilford.

Skovholt, T.M., & Ronnestad, M.H. (1992). Themes in therapist and counselor development. *Journal of Counseling & Development, 70*(4), 505–515.

Stoltenberg, C.D., & McNeill, B.W. (2010). *IDM supervision: An integrative developmental model for supervising counselors and therapists* (3rd ed.). New York: Routledge.

ACKNOWLEDGMENTS

I am thankful to my esteemed colleagues and friends who graciously offered to review this book and provided suggestions for improving it. Dr. Howard Kirschenbaum, one of the leading scholars on Carl Rogers and the Person-Centered Approach, helped me clarify my description and integration of the Person-Centered Approach. Dr. Andre Marquis, who was a close colleague and frequent collaborator with the late Michael Mahoney, assisted me in interpreting Mahoney's Constructive Psychotherapy and applying it to supervision. Unfortunately, Michael Mahoney passed away several years ago, but my hope is that the work is consistent with his vision and ideals. Dr. Richard Ryan, co-founder of Self-Determination Theory (SDT), and Dr. Martin Lynch, a former student of Ryan's and expert in SDT, assisted in clarifying how principles of intrinsic motivation can be utilized in clinical supervision. Dr. Karen Mackie, a narrative therapist and supervisor, helped me think more critically about modernist critiques of narrative approaches and constructivist assessment practices. Dr. David Paré, a renowned expert in narrative and collaborative therapy, assisted in clarifying distinctions between the proposed constructive approach and narrative principles of therapy. Dr. Robert Neimeyer, one of the leading experts in constructivist psychotherapy, provided suggestions for improving my description of constructivist psychotherapeutic processes and in better articulating the historical origins of the approach. Dr. Stephen Demanchick, editor of the *International Journal of Play Therapy*, provided helpful suggestions on integrating humanistic principles into the approach. I am also thankful to Dr. Janine Bernard, a renowned expert in the field of clinical supervision, for her suggestions for improving this work and for her thoughtful and complimentary foreword. Additionally, I am thankful to Tammy Schedlin for her assistance in adding the reference lists to this work.

1

A BRIEF INTRODUCTION TO CONSTRUCTIVIST COUNSELING, DEVELOPMENT, AND LEARNING

I begin this chapter by defining constructivism and briefly outlining the premises of constructivist psychotherapy. I then review several constructivist perspectives regarding human growth and change, beginning with Mahoney's (2006) constructivist model of human change processes. Next I provide an overview of Counselor Development Theory from a constructivist perspective. This is followed by a review of constructivist pedagogical principles, focusing specifically on models that have applied these principles to counselor education. These constructivist views of human growth, development, and learning provide the interpretive foundation for conceptualizing the developmental needs of supervisees and developing supervision interventions from what I will refer to as a *constructive* perspective.

A Brief Introduction to Constructivism

The term "constructivism" comes from the Latin *con struere*, which means *to arrange* or *to build*. Constructivism, therefore, can be conceptualized quite simply as the ongoing act of building or structuring (Mahoney, 2004). The notion of structuring, from a constructivist perspective, arose in direct contrast to *objectivism*, or what is sometimes referred to as *modernism*. Arising from the Enlightenment era, modernists believe in an objective reality in which knowledge exists independent of attempts to observe and understand this knowledge (McAuliffe & Eriksen, 1999). In other words, modernists believe that there is one reality that is the same for everyone, and that this reality can be observed, documented, and presented as truth. Similarly, and perhaps most relevant to counselors and psychotherapists, modernists view the self as a separate, singular entity that exists in isolation to others (Lyddon & Weill, 1997). Early psychologists tended to view the profession through a modernist lens, seeking to observe objective truths about various elements of human activity and to accumulate this information into generalizable truths about the human condition (Neimeyer, 1995).

Postmodern thought arose in opposition to this idea that knowable, observable truths exist. Rather than seeking to identify knowable realities that could be generalized to all humans, postmodernism focused instead on producing localized knowledge that could be understood in context (Neimeyer & Mahoney, 1995). Additionally, postmodernism also viewed the self not as a self-contained, independent entity, but as socially constituted, existing only in relationship to and with others (Lyddon & Weill, 1997). While constructivists vary in their conceptualization of reality, from radical constructivism (von Glasersfeld, 1995), in which there is no ontological reality, to the more critical constructivist approaches that acknowledge an existence of a real world,[1] they all share a common distrust in objective, knowable realities that can be generalized and, instead, place a priority on understanding and validating individual perceptions of reality.

One useful way to illustrate a constructivist perspective of reality is through the concept of *reality tunnels*, which is a term originally coined by Timothy Leary and later popularized by Robert Anton Wilson (1990). According to Wilson (1990), our various human systems (neurological, endocrine, neuromuscular, immunological, etc.) receive over a billion signals every minute from the environment. Because it is impossible to continually pay attention to so many signals (if we did, we would only be able to perceive disorganization and chaos), the nervous system develops "models" (p. 91) to inform decisions about which information is important to recognize and react to, which can safely be disregarded, and what information is too threatening to our worldviews to acknowledge. These models, which are informed both by genetics and by learning and conditioning (particularly early learning experiences), are what ultimately decide what stimuli people attend to and the meaning they make of it, thus shaping their conceptualizations of *reality*. While there may be a *reality* out there, it is impossible for any two people to view it in exactly the same way because each person's *reality tunnel* is unique. From this perspective, it is impossible to make assertions about *a* reality; all we can describe are comparative realities.

To illustrate the idea of *reality tunnels*, Wilson (2005) described an experiment he conducted hundreds of times with participants at his various talks and workshops. At some point during the talk, he would ask people in the audience to describe the hallway outside the seminar room. In conducting this experiment for nearly forty years with hundreds of people, Wilson asserted that nobody ever described the hallway in the exact same way, and often they described it drastically differently. While everyone entered through the exact same hallway, each person attended to slightly different stimuli and interpreted it in different ways based on their unique reality tunnels, thus creating multiple realities of the hallway.

In addition to sharing a common distrust in objective, knowable realities, Mahoney (2006) has summarized several other overarching principles shared by most constructivists. First, like existentialists, constructivists believe humans are active participants or *agents* in their own lives who must pay close attention to the flow of life activity. Second, constructivists share a belief that humans need order to organize their worlds and that they create meaning based on these systems of order. Third, our systems of ordering are constantly changing and emerging as we interact with the world. Constructivism, therefore, recognizes and honors a personal identity, or *self*, from a phenomenological perspective. Fourth, constructivists share a belief that we have an inherent need to form relationships with others and that much of the order we make of the world results from interpersonal relationships. The self, therefore, does not exist in isolation and cannot be understood without consideration of the social-symbolic systems to which it is a part. Finally, constructivists share an assumption that all these processes combine to form a dynamic process of dialectical development in which people constantly struggle between order, disorder, and reorder.

According to Mahoney (2006), these ideas regarding humans as actively constructing and continually reconstructing meaning date as far back as the 6th century BC to the teachings of Lao Tzu, who articulated the need for humans to embrace change and life's opposite forces (yin and yang) in the writings of the Tao. The ideas were also central in the teachings of the Buddha (560–477 BC) and in the pre-socratic philosophy of Heraclitus (540–470 BC). However, more recent writers often credited as the originators of the modern ideas of constructivism are Giambattista Vico (1668–1744), Immanuel Kant (1724–1804), Arthur Schopenhauer (1788–1860), and Hans Vaihinger (1852–1933).[2]

Constructivist ideas are also apparent in many of the major theories of psychotherapy, most notably in the works of Alfred Adler, Albert Bandura, Gregory Bateson, Jerome Bruner, James Bugental, Vikton Frankl, and William James. Additionally, Jean Piaget's work examining children's cognitive development, in particular, the dynamic process of assimilation and accommodation that allows children to integrate what is novel with what is known, is considered central to constructivist learning theory. According to Mahoney (2006), Piaget's emphasis that we "organize our worlds by organizing ourselves" continues to strongly influence constructivist views of development.

Most recently, constructivist ideas have been prominently integrated into systems of psychotherapy by scholars such as Robert Neimeyer, William Lyddon, Vittorio Guidano, and the aforementioned Michael Mahoney. The perspectives these authors have taken regarding constructivist psychotherapy were heavily influenced by the work of George Kelly (1955), who developed a system of personality based on constructivist thinking. Kelly termed this constructivist theory of personality *Personal Construct Theory*, and outlined an approach to psychotherapy that allowed counselors to understand and carefully challenge the ways in which clients construct their views of themselves and their relationships with others. Kelly believed that people are inherently driven toward action and movement and asserted that the counselor's role was to help clients understand this movement by deconstructing their personal constructs, or meanings they have made about the world, themselves, and others. This process of observing one's own interpretations of the world in order to understand one's actions and chart a new course of action was a process that Kelly believed to be never ending. Therefore, rather than attempting to help clients *solve* this cognitive puzzle for the purpose of feeling stable and secure in the world, Kelly helped clients embrace the anxiety of living in a forever unstable and dynamic world. Instead of helping clients retreat to the perceived safety of their familiar personal constructs, Kelly encouraged clients to abandon their previous, outdated personal constructs, and openly embrace the fear and resistance that is inherent when reinventing new ways of viewing the world and their place in this world (Neimeyer, 2009).

In summarizing the main goal shared by constructivist psychotherapists such as George Kelly, Neimeyer (2009) stated that constructivist therapy "is more a matter of *intervening in meaning* than it is a procedure for ameliorating unwanted symptoms or training people in more adequate coping skills" (p. 5). This recognition regarding the importance of individual meaning-making processes forms the basis of the constructivist approach to supervision that I will outline in this book. However, before beginning to describe the actual process of constructive supervision, it is important to outline constructivist perspectives of development and change, as these perspectives provide the lens through which supervisors can conceptualize the process and goals of supervision.

Constructivist Perspectives on Development, Growth, and Change

The facilitation of client development is widely regarded as the primary goal of counseling from a constructivist perspective (e.g., Ivey & Goncalves, 1988; Steenbarger, 1991). As a result, constructivists have developed eloquent ways of understanding human growth and change in clients as a means of fostering client success. In much the same way, a constructivist view of supervision also places development, in this case, supervisee development, at the center of the supervision process for facilitating change and growth in supervisees. This is not to minimize the importance of monitoring client welfare and professional gatekeeping to clinical supervision; however, these important functions of supervision are arguably honored and upheld when supervisors focus intensively on the developmental progression of their supervisees (see Chapter 6 for a more detailed discussion of the role of gatekeeping and monitoring in constructive supervision). Constructivist developmental theory can allow supervisors to use traditional theories of supervision more effectively and in ways that account for supervisees' constructions of the world in the same way that these developmental theories are used by constructivist psychotherapists to facilitate client change in therapy. Supervisors who view their supervisees through the lens of constructivist developmental theory are able to understand the complex experiences of their supervisees, normalize rather than pathologize difficult aspects of change for supervisees, and provide interventions that are suited to their supervisees' individual developmental needs.

While counselors and supervisors alike widely recognize the prominent role of developmental theory in counseling and supervision, Steenbarger (1991) has noted that a large percentage of the theories of human development utilized by counselors are stage theories that are based on an organismic worldview in which individuals are involved in a process of "maturational unfolding" (p. 288). This idea about development has derived, to a large extent, from Erikson's (1968) seminal theory of psychosocial development, which is based on the epigenetic principle. Borrowed from the field of embryology, the principle asserts that all things develop based on an inherent ground plan that arises from within the organism. According to Erikson (1968), each part of a person's psychological development has its own special time for "ascendancy" until all parts have risen to form a whole (p. 92). Inherent in this principle is the idea that development is sequential, meaning that individuals must pass through certain stages that occur during specified age ranges in order to proceed through later stages of development.

According to Steenbarger (1991), stage theories are appealing to counselors because they provide a predictable sequence with which to view human change and an optimistic view of the potential for individuals to develop and grow. However, there are also a number of salient shortcomings to stage theories of human development. Because of the emphasis on linearity, stage theories often fail to account for the more complex, and often non-linear elements of human development. Second, stage theories, while often recognizing the role of social interactions in the process of development, fail to emphasize the interactional nature of these person/environment interactions. Third, stage theories often fail to account for cultural differences, sometimes even going as far as pathologizing developmental diversity. These salient critiques regarding the limitations of developmental theory have led some within the constructivist psychotherapy movement (most notably, those within the narrative tradition) to eschew all theories of human development (Crocket, 2004).

Rather than abandoning the use of developmental theory, other constructivist psychotherapists have asserted alternative views of development which provide counselors with more contextualized perspectives. Instead of viewing development as occurring only in static, linear sequences, constructivist theories of development can provide counselors and supervisors with innovative and applied contextual views of personality, learning, and change. In contrast to organismic or stage theories of development, constructivist theories of development (1) prioritize an understanding of development in cultural and historical contexts, (2) emphasize process over content (i.e., end stages), and (3) do not view equilibrium as the developmental ideal. Instead, a constructivist view of development prioritizes change as a developmental norm and seeks to assist people in embracing rather than resisting change.

One of the most eloquent models for describing human growth and change from a developmental–constructivist perspective was offered by Michael Mahoney. While Mahoney conducted numerous studies on human change and published a detailed book on human change processes from a constructivist lens (see Mahoney, 1991), he was also able to condense this elaborate theory into a straightforward and parsimonious model for use by psychotherapists. Although the model is designed to understand processes of change in clients participating in psychotherapy, it also lends itself to understanding how supervisees develop and change during the course of clinical supervision and, as a result, can assist supervisors in understanding the developmental needs of their supervisees.

Mahoney's (2006) constructivist model of human change is based on three primary assumptions: (a) that humans can change, (b) that humans can help one another in the process of changing, and (c) that some human interaction patterns are more helpful than others in facilitating human change processes. While it is the third assumption (i.e., how to help supervisees change) that will be the primary focus of this book, it is also important to understand the basic elements of change outlined by Mahoney in order to understand how to best facilitate necessary changes in supervision.

Mahoney asserted that while humans always desire balanced states, learning and growth only occur when we fall out of balance. From this perspective, order is not preferential for development: both order and disorder are needed for healthy, normal development. According to Mahoney, the need for change can become apparent when people experience prolonged and unexplained feelings of sadness, anxiousness, or anger; or encounter changes in previously stable patterns such as sleeping and eating. Unlike some other psychological theories that may attempt to isolate, label, and treat difficult emotions or changes in life patterns as "problems," constructivists view these disturbances as "natural expressions of a life that is trying to reorganize itself" (Mahoney, 2006, p. 8). Sleeplessness or prolonged periods of unexplained sadness, for example, would not be viewed as problems to be treated by constructivists; rather, they are seen as indicators or signs that change is needed. Treating a symptom like sleeplessness, from a constructivist perspective, would be analogous to a driver attempting to cover up or dismantle the "check engine" light in his car when it comes on rather than conducting a more detailed diagnostic check to determine the problem with the vehicle that caused the "check engine" light to come on.

Mahoney (2006) also noted, however, that people inherently resist change because it can be uncomfortable. To stick with my "check engine" light analogy, some people would prefer to just cover up or dismantle the "check engine" light rather than acknowledge that there is really something wrong with the car that will require a detailed diagnostic examination and, perhaps, costly and time-consuming maintenance. Constructivists understand that change is difficult and that we, as humans, are fundamentally conservative creatures who strive for continuity and structure (Mahoney, 2006). The constructive supervisor understands that supervisees may, at times, cling to existing ways of knowing, even when they have identified limitations to these existing approaches. In fact, some supervisees may be downright defensive as they struggle to consider limitations of their established ways of understanding and relating to clients. Resistance to change often manifests in the use of defense mechanisms like denial, aggressiveness, or helplessness. Constructive supervisors understand that resistance, anxiety, and even defensiveness are normal behaviors and do not seek to pathologize such behaviors or to battle them. Rather, they seek to join with supervisees in ways that help them observe and understand these processes of disequilibrium and resistance as they occur. Rather than being surprised by defensive posturing by supervisees during supervision, constructivist supervisors recognize and even expect these behaviors as normal elements of the human change process. Instead of quickly labeling supervisees who demonstrate defensive postures during supervision as "pathological" or "unfit for the field," constructivists seek to empathically join with the supervisee to understand the origins and purposes of the defensive positions.

Mahoney also cautioned that while supported periods of disorder are needed for growth to occur, big falls, or periods of drastic and sustained disorder which are unsupported, can overwhelm people and cause harm. At the same time constructive supervisors facilitate complex change processes in supervisees, they also recognize and allow change to slow down when supervisees feel overwhelmed by too much change. In describing the complexity involved in assisting clients in this process during psychotherapy, Mahoney (2006) offered the metaphor of "*opening and closing*" (p. 24). Like therapy, the supervision session is a dynamic encounter in which the supervisee is constantly opening and closing to experiences, ideas, and new ways of thinking. When supervisees are open, they expand their understandings by becoming accepting of new ways of thinking and being. These experiences of opening are often followed by periods of closing off, even retracting. Mahoney has asserted that this process prevents people from changing more rapidly than their inner or outer systems can accommodate at that time. Mahoney cautioned that neither opening nor closing are inherently good or bad, but merely different sides of the same coin: both are necessary for change. Moreover, both processes can occur simultaneously in different areas and in different ways. In the case of supervision, a supervisee might be open in one regard, like conceptualizing client issues in a new way, while, at the same time, appear closed to exploring their personal understanding of their own life course issue. While constructive supervisors regularly facilitate supervisee *opening*, they are also acutely aware of the need for supervisees to retract from time to time and they seek to assist them in balancing this complex change process.

Mahoney (1991) also asserted that human knowing results from the interplay between what he labeled *feedback* and *feedforward* mechanisms. Feedforward mechanisms are thoughts that allow us to anticipate things (events, reactions, etc.) in order to provide predictability and stability in an otherwise unpredictable world. When these feedforward, or anticipated response mechanisms are violated, people are forced to initiate feedback mechanisms that allow them to adapt to the novel situations they have encountered. It is through the feedback process, Mahoney asserted, where new learning and growth occurs. Problems arise, however, when feedforward mechanisms are maintained despite their inappropriateness or lack of viability for current situations.

Mahoney also observed that if a challenge persists, people will often realize the need to deviate from their established patterns of thinking and behaving and, thus, begin a process of disorganizing these prior patterns. It is in this process of disorganization that supervisors are most effective in helping supervisees reorganize by supporting them as they consider new, more fitting ways of being in the world or in relating to clients. Ultimately, Mahoney's theory, when applied to supervision, suggests that supervisees can shift from an old order that is becoming increasingly unable to handle new circumstances, to a new order that is more responsive to their surroundings.

In addition to Mahoney's developmental–constructivist model of change, there are additional theories that have explored developmental change processes in counselors and counselors-in-training and that provide an important lens from which to view human change processes in supervision from a constructivist perspective. These theories of counselor development will be reviewed below.

Developmental–Constructivist Models of Counselor Development

One recently developed model designed to understand change and growth among counselor education students from a constructivist framework was developed by Garrett McAuliffe. McAuliffe's (2011) model is based on Piaget's (1954) Theory of Cognitive Development, along with the perspectives of other influential developmental theorists such as Kegan (1998), Kohlberg (1969), and Perry (1998). The focus of McAuliffe's model is on understanding how counseling students' overall approaches to knowing can evolve from "more rigid, authoritarian ways of knowing to more flexible, open, and reflective ones" (p. 6). McAuliffe illustrates this process of knowing by delineating different stages that people go through as they acquire new knowledge. Like other developmental–constructivist approaches, McAuliffe recognized limitations of stage theories and cautions readers that these stages are not absolute and can vary by time and situation. While students generally have dominant ways of knowing that center around the particular stage in which they are located, McAuliffe asserted that they do not rely solely on this one way of knowing in every situation. Although students might gravitate toward constructing knowledge in a way consistent with a certain stage, other ways of knowing that are consistent with other stages may also be available to them at certain times depending on a number of contextual factors.

McAuliffe delineated three overall ways of knowing that are particularly important for understanding how students acquire knowledge as they are engaged in formal counseling training. The first stage is termed *received/conventional knowing*. Counseling students characterized by this stage tend to see the world as fixed and their cultural norms as absolute truths. As a result, they rely largely on external forms of knowledge when conceptualizing clients. Supervisees in this stage may regularly seek to solicit direct advice from the supervisor and regular assessment regarding their performance to make sure they are getting it right. These students may have a harder time initially developing answers on their own or justifying how they know certain things about clients and will have intense struggles during periods of ambiguity. They also show a difficult time challenging established hierarchies, even those that are unresponsive to non-dominant groups (McAuliffe & Lovell, 2006).

The second stage of knowing outlined by McAuliffe (2011) is *self-authorized knowing*. In this stage, students begin to experience limitations to their received/conventional ways of knowing, which causes them to begin to more comfortably question and challenge more established ways of knowing. They also begin to use their own judgment more in formulating ideas and decisions, recognizing that knowledge varies according to context. They begin, therefore, to pull away from relying on one particular expert, theory, or literature base and start seeking answers by critically evaluating a wide range of information and alternative ways of thinking. McAuliffe and Lovell (2006) have found that counselors who are characterized by the self-authorized knowing stage are more likely to demonstrate client empathy, self-reflection, and insight than those in the received/conventional knowing stage. One limitation, however, is that counselors in this stage can become overly guided by their own logic and become dismissive of other more established and, at times, complete sources of information. Supervisees in this stage may, therefore, resist suggestions from supervisors to look to the literature for answers or dismiss advice from their instructors or supervisors.

The third stage outlined by McAuliffe is *dialectical knowing*. In this stage, counseling students are able to understand the world by engaging and critiquing multiple (even dichotomous) perspectives and are even able to regularly question the certainty of their own understandings by considering views that are in opposition to their own. They recognize that they are constantly engaged in the process of knowledge construction and are self-conscious and aware of their own thoughts, emotions, and reactions to new information. They have an ability to deeply understand the perspectives of others and to feel connected to others, even if they do not agree with their perspectives. Likewise, they recognize the inevitability of conflict and are able to engage in conflict in ways that allow others and themselves to grow, as opposed to avoiding conflict at all costs or engaging in conflict in ways that are harmful. As a result of their connectedness with others, people in this stage typically are sensitive to the needs of others and seek to be socially engaged in ways that promote well-being.

In applying these developmental–constructivist stages to counselor training, McAuliffe asserted that counselor educators should regularly seek to "trigger dilemmas that call into question students' received views about what is good and right" (p. 11) and then provide opportunities for them to reflect on these experiences in meaningful ways to foster professional growth. Given that the more advanced ways of knowing seem to correspond with counselor competence (McAuliffe & Lovell, 2006), one might envision progression on stages such as these as appropriate outcomes for supervision.

In addition to McAuliffe's developmental–constructivist approach to understanding how counseling students develop during their training, there are also theories that have examined counselor/supervisee development more broadly and beyond their experiences as students. These models of counseling development, while sharing several developmental dimensions with McAuliffe's model (especially in the student phases), provide a more detailed and nuanced view of the developmental progression of supervisees at various points of their professional development. Unlike McAuliffe, these developmental theories were not developed specifically from a constructivist perspective; however, they provide another valuable lens for understanding the complex developmental processes in supervisees when considered from a constructivist lens.

While there are over twenty counselor/supervisee developmental models that have been described in professional literature (Bernard & Goodyear, 2014), two of the most cited and empirically supported of these theories are the Integrated Developmental Model (IDM; Stoltenberg & McNeil, 2010) and Skovholt and Ronnestad's (1992) Theory of Counselor Development. While each theory provides some unique elements to understanding how supervisees change throughout the process of supervision, the models also share much in common. Below I provide a summary of counselor development in which I have integrated salient elements of both of these established, empirically supported models in order to present a more general view of supervisee developmental processes.

Counselor development literature indicates that all counselors begin their initial counseling training with predisposed ideas of how problems occur and what their role is as a helper based upon their experiences in helping friends, relatives, colleagues, etc. through difficult situations. Often these predisposed notions include behaviors that are inconsistent with professional counseling skills, such as rushing to solve the problem before fully understanding it, giving advice, or seeking to cheer people up by minimizing the problem. The incongruency between their predisposed ideas of helping and the professional skills they learn in graduate school can cause new counselors to feel anxious and overwhelmed as they seek to integrate new professional skills with their predisposed notions of helping. Some counselor trainees may even attempt to assess their level of fit with the field based upon the extent to which their predisposed notions of helping align with the professional theories and skills they learn in their training.

New counseling students also begin their training with extremely high levels of motivation to learn; but, this motivation is often overly focused toward learning the "right" way to counsel. As a result, supervisees in their early practicum and or internship experiences are often extremely uncomfortable with the high level of ambiguity that is inherent in the profession and will often seek straightforward answers and advice from instructors, supervisors, and professional literature, which they will attempt to generalize to all situations. For example, a beginning supervisee may receive feedback from a supervisor that her self-disclosure with a client appeared to place the focus of the interaction on the counselor rather than on her client. Upon receiving that feedback, the counselor trainee may attempt to generalize this feedback as "okay, I should never self-disclose because it takes the focus off the client," despite the fact that she has read literature or heard in lectures about the appropriate use of self-disclosure in psychotherapy.

Their high levels of motivation can also contribute to high levels of anxiety about their performance, especially with regard to the feedback and evaluations they receive from their supervisors and clients. In fact, they may attempt to only share with supervisors the experiences in which they feel they have succeeded while hiding from them instances in which they feel they were less successful or have made mistakes. The anxiety they experience regarding evaluation can also cause new counselors to focus more on their own performances during sessions rather than focusing on their clients, which can cause them to miss a lot of what clients say. It is not uncommon, for example, for a new counseling student to fail to notice salient client statements during a session or to notice them only upon reviewing a tape or transcript later. Newer trainees also tend to have strong emotional connections to their clients but may have a difficult time regulating their own emotional involvement and, consequently, separating themselves from these emotional connections.

As supervisees gain more experience through participation in internships, they begin to function more autonomously, relying more on their own internal judgment and less on external sources (such as supervisors) when conceptualizing clients and deciding upon interventions. They also begin to more critically evaluate their sources of professional influence, selectively integrating advice, theories, etc. that they like while disregarding sources of information that fail to mesh with their evolving professional identity. In fact, some may show resistance to supervisor suggestions at this point as they attempt to establish their own counseling identity. At the same time, prior successes with clients may cause them to have elevated expectations of themselves and, as a result, they can place a great deal of pressure on themselves to work perfectly with all their clients. This can manifest in excessively thorough attention to details or extreme cautiousness in their approaches at the expense of spontaneity, creativity, and enjoyment. There is also the potential for students in this stage to have more self-awareness regarding their own reactions to their clients.

Once students graduate from their professional training programs and begin their first professional counseling positions, Skovholt and Ronnestad (1992) note that they can demonstrate a strong need to validate what they learned in their professional training, which is followed by a period of disillusionment with this training once they encounter challenges for which their graduate training did not prepare them. Such professional disillusionment can be particularly difficult for counselors who relied exclusively on one particular theoretical approach during their graduate training (who Skovholt and Ronnestad refer to as "true believers"). This tension between validating and criticizing their professional training leads to an intense period of self-exploration regarding their professional skills and identity, which can include participating in their own counseling as a client. While this period is often filled with tension and ambiguity as they seek to develop their own, autonomous styles, this phase also includes growing confidence in their own instincts, the integration of their own "personalities" into their professional work, and the ability to establish effective work roles and boundaries.

Later in their careers, after gaining experience with a wide variety of client issues, seasoned counselors often strive to develop a counseling approach that is congruent with their personal values and attitudes about the world. While this can translate into finding a new approach that is already established in the literature, more often it involves moving away from relying on established theories and focusing instead on self-knowledge gained through their own experiences. In fact, many seasoned practitioners will abandon more rigid and formulaic approaches in favor of being more creative. Experienced counselors may also look to sources outside of the psychotherapy literature when exploring new ways of conceptualizing client issues and formulating interventions, which can include religious, biographical, and even fictional literature.

Counselor Development Theory can be central in assisting constructive supervisors in normalizing supervisee experiences which might seem problematic if they were to manifest in other situations. One example of this occurred in a small group session in which I was providing supervision to a group of supervisors (i.e., supervision of supervision). During the session, a supervisor (Mary) described her experience working with a beginning masters level practicum student who was presenting one of her early counseling sessions to her. At one point during the supervision session, the supervisee began describing feelings of anxiety about "doing it right" and being viewed as competent by Mary. The supervisee also reported getting anxious with her client to the point that she actually dissuaded him from talking about his problem in great detail (a goal she had established in a previous session) because she did not want him to feel bad. At this point, some of the other supervisors in the small group session began expressing concern about the supervisee, some even going as far as questioning the supervisee's fit with the field. Counselors, they argued, need to be comfortable with client emotion and should not put their own needs for competence above the needs of the client.

After listening to the concerns of her fellow supervisors, Mary, who identifies with constructivist ideas and was well-versed in counselor development literature, replied to the group that she believed her supervisee was not only experiencing normal issues for a new counselor, but was also actually advanced in her ability not only to recognize these issues, but also to verbalize these feelings to her supervisor. Armed with this developmental perspective, Mary was then able to develop an intervention that focused on helping the supervisee explore more deeply her feelings of insecurity, need to "get it right," and fear of client emotion. The next session, the supervisee had what Mary referred to as a "breakthrough" with herself and her client.

An understanding of human change processes and counselor development from a constructivist perspective is crucial to the constructive approach to clinical supervision. These developmental–constructivist perspectives on human growth and change allow supervisors a holistic lens from which to view their supervisees' experiences and transitions during supervision. There are, however, additional constructivist models that are essential to conceptualizing the process of supervision from a constructive framework. In the next section I will describe how constructivist theories of learning, particularly those that have been applied to counselor education pedagogical practices, can provide another important means for understanding how supervisors can effectively facilitate supervisee development, growth, and change from a constructivist perspective.

A Constructivist Approach to Counselor Education

In an earlier paper (Guiffrida, 2005), I offered an *Emergence Model* for teaching theories of counseling from a constructivist pedagogical framework. The model was based on a thorough review and integration of a number of constructivist-based pedagogical theories, including reflective-based pedagogy (Argyris & Schon, 1974; Schon, 1995), radical constructivist pedagogy (von Glasersfeld, 1995), adult theories of learning (Mezirow, 1997), and spiritual/transformative pedagogies (Campbell, 2001; Krishnamurti, 1953; Miller, 2001). While the model was specifically designed to help counseling students discover their inherent theoretical orientations, these same constructivist principles of learning can also be applied to the practice of supervision and form a core component of the constructive approach to clinical supervision. These principles include the notions that (1) knowledge must be discovered rather than imparted from teacher to student; (2) learning is influenced not only by the current learning experiences, but also by predisposed notions derived from their prior experiences; (3) language is central not only in communicating discoveries, but also in the process of discovery itself; and (4) some anxiety and mistakes are necessary in discovering new knowledge. Below I will provide a brief description of each of these constructivist principles of learning and an overview of how they can be applied to the process of constructive supervision.[3]

The core of constructivism is the belief that knowledge is subjective and varies depending on the mental construction of each observer (McAuliffe & Eriksen, 1999). Constructive supervisors, therefore, recognize that there is not one *right* way to conduct counseling. While there are certainly approaches that are *wrong*, meaning they are unethical and/or pose potential harm to clients, constructive supervisors recognize there are countless *right ways* depending upon the client, counselor, and contextual factors. Rather than expecting supervisees to adhere to the supervisor's approach, constructive supervision empowers supervisees to develop their own answers that are right for them. In highlighting the centrality of knowledge construction to the process of constructivist psychotherapy, Greg Neimeyer (1995) stated:

> Gone is the certainty of a single "best", "right", or functional focus of thinking, feeling, and behaving. Gone too is the directive, disputational comportment associated with that certainty, replaced by a more tentative, patient struggle aimed at developing a constructive process of exploration from within the individual that may lead to a more viable and developmentally progressive understanding of the world.
>
> (p. 113)

While Neimeyer's statement was written about clients in psychotherapy, it also beautifully captures the essence of the constructive approach to supervision.

Similarly, constructivists hold that knowledge is not something that can be imparted from teacher to student (or, in our case, supervisor to supervisee). Rather, they believe that learning occurs best when the learner is engaged in individual and social activity that promotes discovery. Constructive supervisors, therefore, do not focus on transferring their own knowledge to their supervisees in the form of lecturing, modeling, etc. Rather, they seek primarily to provide the space in which knowledge can be discovered by their supervisees. Lecturing and advice giving, from a constructivist perspective, provide the potential to limit critical thinking and reflexivity among supervisees and can breed dependency on the supervisor for answers (Guiffrida, 2005). This is not to say that a constructive supervisor refrains completely from teaching or giving advice; teaching and advice are, however, used much more sparingly and carefully when operating from a constructive approach when compared to more traditional approaches to supervision.[4]

Constructivists also hold that learning is influenced not only by the current learning experiences, but also by predisposed notions derived from their prior experiences. In other words, constructivists are acutely aware of the fact that supervisees arrive in supervision with predisposed notions of human growth and change, even those who are brand new to the field. Rather than disregarding these predisposed notions or attempting to replace them with their own more informed notions, a constructive supervisor seeks to understand all forms of supervisee knowledge so that supervisees can understand how these ingrained thought patterns impact current learning processes.

Constructivists also value the critical role of language to the learning process. However, rather than using language primarily to convey knowledge from the instructor to the students, constructivists argue that language is a tool that should be used by students to convey their discoveries and understanding of the phenomenon. Further, constructivists believe that it is through the narrative process (i.e., thinking about an experience, critically evaluating it, organizing it into logical frameworks, and creating words to express it) that knowledge is actually created. A constructivist supervisor, therefore, seeks to provide space for supervisees to reflect upon and actively construct counseling knowledge.

This fundamental tenet regarding the construction of knowledge is an aspect of constructive supervision that many supervisors, even those who espouse humanistic approaches to therapy, often have a difficult time fully accepting and implementing in supervision. Most supervisors, after all, have attained their positions as supervisors because they are experienced and competent counselors. With experience and demonstrated competence there naturally come preferred ways of conducting counseling, including specific conceptualizations of how counselors should relate to clients, conceptualize their problems, and intervene. As a result, it can be difficult for these seasoned experts to refrain from imposing their own ways of doing things on their supervisees, especially when the supervisees themselves are very willing to absorb this knowledge from their supervisors. Even Carl Rogers, perhaps the best-known proponent regarding the benefits of clients discovering their own answers in therapy, was quoted as stating that he sometimes, as a supervisor, felt the urge to ask the supervisee to "Move out of that chair" so that he could "take over" (Hackney & Goodyear, 1984, p. 285). It is understandable, therefore, that other supervisors, including but not limited to those who are not adherent to these humanistic principles in their work as counselors, might also struggle in allowing supervisees to discover their own answers.

One reason that supervisors often give for their lack of patience in providing space for supervisees to discover their own answers in supervision relates to perceptions about the need to "protect" clients. Certainly, supervisors must protect clients from harm and need to actively intervene when they observe unethical or irresponsible counselor behaviors that may lead to harm. New counselors can, for example, fail to properly identify homicidal/suicidal ideations in clients (despite receiving training in these areas) or to intervene properly when they do identify these situations. Other instances of potential client harm that necessitate action by the supervisor can include supervisors noticing inappropriate dual relationships between clients and counselors or counselors who are implementing risky interventions that may be unsettling to vulnerable clients.[5] In these instances, the constructive supervisor must actively intervene by providing direct advice and/or alerting authorities or others involved with the supervisee or the site to which they are working.

However, supervisors can often use this same rationale of "protecting clients" as a reason to teach supervisees their own ways of doing things rather than allowing supervisees to construct their own approaches. Specifically, this can happen when supervisors witness supervisees acting in ways that are safe and ethical, but are *different* than the ways the supervisor would have preceded. Often, the supervisor will feel their direct intervening in the form of teaching and advice giving is needed because the counselor is not proceeding in a manner that they perceive to be as efficient or valuable to clients as their own preferred approach. This more directed approach to supervision, however, provides the potential of stifling supervisee growth and development, which ultimately can prove less helpful to the clients than had the supervisee been allowed to develop their own answers in a more reflective manner. Rather than trying to get supervisees to learn and understand the supervisor's ways of viewing client problems and interventions, constructive supervisors engage supervisees in a process of critical self-reflection that allows supervisees to openly express their thoughts, feelings, and inclinations regarding their clients in ways that facilitate critical examination of the strengths, limitations, and origins of these beliefs. Through this process of open examination, supervisees are often able to develop sophisticated understandings of themselves and their clients that are consistent with their own predisposed notions of growth and development.

Supervisors can also struggle with allowing supervisees to discover their own answers because of inherent needs to demonstrate competence. New supervisors, even those who are seasoned professional counselors, are often nervous about beginning the process of supervision. Much of this fear stems from the fact that they are insecure about their own knowledge of counseling. None of us know everything there is to know about this incredibly dynamic profession and the chances are that the supervisee will bring an issue or question that is not within the realm of expertise of the supervisor.

This fear of being seen by supervisees as incompetent became apparent to me a few years ago during a group supervision session of a new supervisor. In her session, which we were watching on videotape, the supervisor was strictly located in the role of a teacher (providing direct advice, complimenting, evaluating, etc.) and had not provided any space for her supervisee to find her own answers. From the supervisor's perspective, the supervisee was progressing in a way she thought was productive and, according to the supervisor, was enjoying her experience greatly in supervision. The other members of the supervision group, however, questioned whether the supervisor was fostering dependency on her by providing so much advice and evaluation and not allowing the supervisee to find her own voice. The supervisor became angry at this question, eventually stating in a harsh tone, "If she can just do it all herself, why does she need me?"

Rather than lecturing to this supervisor about the importance of the supervisee having space to find her own answers, I chose to ask her the following question that helped her clarify her feelings toward her supervisee: Why is it important for you to be needed and helpful in this way with her? That question, in this case and in subsequent cases since then, has been helpful in allowing supervisors-in-training to explore how their own needs may impact the roles they take in supervision. After some initial resistance, which included statements like "It's my obligation to her," the supervisor began to articulate how some of her own needs were also being met through her active, instructive approach. In her case, she disclosed that she had always felt like she was not good enough, in prior educational environments and her personal life, and that she wanted to prove to her supervisee and to herself that she was knowledgeable. In this case, the question helped the supervisor to reflect upon her need to be in control and to serve as an expert for her supervisee. Armed with this self-awareness, she then became more open to and comfortable with her supervisee becoming the expert during supervision.

Also central to the constructivist approach to learning is the unique constructivist view regarding the role of anxiety in learning. Many traditional approaches to supervision are based on behaviorist principles of learning, which hold that anxiety is something that gets in the way of learning (see Bandura, 1997). As a result, behaviorist approaches seek to reduce anxiety and build self-efficacy by carefully scaffolding experiences to reduce the number of problems that supervisees encounter. Some supervisors will even insist that their supervisees spend their early training experiences observing the supervisor as he or she provides psychotherapy to his or her own clients. From a behaviorist perspective, this type of *modeling* reduces anxiety and builds self-efficacy.

As described earlier in this chapter, constructivists do not view moderate amounts of supervisee anxiety and discomfort as problematic to effective learning. In fact, constructivists believe that some discomfort is necessary to facilitate change processes. Whereas a behaviorist approach would seek to reduce supervisee anxiety by providing advice, modeling, or compliments, the constructive supervisor seeks to empathically join with supervisees in ways that allow them to become aware of and comfortable with the anxiety and discomfort they experience as they consider limitations to their prior ways of knowing. Rather than attempting to alleviate anxiety, constructive supervisors encourage and teach their supervisees to embrace anxiety as a necessary condition to their professional development.

Similarly, the constructive supervisor also values and honors supervisee mistakes as central to the learning process. Contrary to the behaviorist perspective of self-efficacy, which asserts that practice experiences should be carefully scaffolded to minimize or eliminate surprises or mistakes (which would lower self-efficacy), constructive supervisors believe that the only true learning occurs when supervisees are confronted by surprises and make mistakes. Rather than trying to prevent or minimize supervisee mistakes, the constructive supervisor seeks to help supervisees normalize these experiences so that they can openly reflect upon them rather than try to hide them or explain them away. It is only through this iterative process of surprise (and sometimes mistakes) and reflection that new knowledge is meaningfully acquired.

The centrality of self-reflection to successful practice was highlighted by Schon (1995), who noted two types of reflection that allow practitioners to continually develop and grow. The first, titled *reflection in-action*, is the process by which practitioners implement knowledge from prior learning to adapt to new, unique situations. This process begins when any experience or performance is interrupted by a surprise, which triggers reflection. At the same time the practitioner is asking him or herself what has occurred, he or she is also reframing the problem and formulating new strategies to overcome it. The process of reflection in-action occurs as the practitioner implements the new intervention based on past learning while also evaluating it and adapting it based on new information from the current experience. Schon (1995) has stated "the actor reflects in action in the sense that his thinking occurs in an action present—a stretch of time within which it is still possible to make a difference to the outcomes of action" (p. 30). This is the process that a good teacher goes through in helping answer a student's difficult question or that a doctor engages in when s/he encounters a patient with a problem that is not in the book. According to Schon, reflection in action is central to the art "by which practitioners sometimes deal with situations of uncertainty, instability, uniqueness, and value conflict" (p. 50).

The second type of *reflection* noted by Schon as necessary for learning to occur from practice is termed *reflection on-action*. Unlike reflection in-action, which occurs in the moment, reflection on-action occurs after the experience has occurred. This is the process by which practitioners evaluate and critique their past performances, linking them to other past performances, and coming to new conclusions or future directions. For counselors, this process occurs most regularly when writing case notes, participating in case conferences with colleagues, and, most relevant to our discussion, during supervision. From a constructivist perspective, the ability to self-reflect is considered *the* most important element to successful counseling. As a result, a constructive approach to supervision places supervisee reflection at the center of the supervision process.

Chapter Summary

While there are many contemporary variations of constructivism, most constructivists share the belief that knowledge is subjective and varies depending upon the experiences of each individual. A constructive approach to supervision centralizes the subjective nature of reality. Additionally, constructive supervisors carry a deep appreciation for and understanding of the complex change processes that supervisees experience during the dynamic process of clinical supervision. While constructive supervisors understand that supervisees must change during the process of supervision, they also recognize that humans inherently resist change. Constructive supervisors, therefore, seek to support supervisees as they engage in this complex change process by facilitating supervisee growth and change while also allowing change to slow or even briefly revert back to prior ways of being when change is perceived as occurring too rapidly.

Constructive supervisors also understand models of counselor development and use these models to assist them in understanding the needs of their supervisees and in developing appropriate interventions. Developmental approaches to constructive supervision can involve normalizing what supervisees perceive as demanding challenges to their growth or empathically joining with them as they struggle to consider limitations of prior ways of conceptualizing their helping roles. Additionally, constructive supervisors facilitate change by fostering supervisee self-reflection through the use of constructivist principles of learning.

Together, these understandings of development, change, and learning form the interpretive lens from which to view the process of supervision from a constructive perspective and to provide a starting point for considering interventions. In the next chapter I will describe how these constructivist principles can be integrated with salient theories of counseling and psychotherapy to form the theoretical basis of the constructive approach to clinical supervision.

Notes

1 See Mahoney (1988) for a detailed review of the debate regarding these stances of reality within constructivist literature.
2 Readers are encouraged to review Mahoney's (2006) book for a more detailed review regarding the history of constructivism and constructivist psychotherapy.
3 See Guiffrida (2005) for a more detailed discussion of these constructivist pedagogical principles.
4 See the Self-Determination Theory section in Chapter 2 for a more detailed discussion on the role of advice in constructive supervision.
5 Readers are encouraged to review Bernard and Goodyear (2014) for a detailed discussion of ethical and legal issues in supervision.

References

Argyris, C., & Schon, D.A. (1974). *Theory in practice: Increasing professional effectiveness.* San Francisco: Jossey-Bass.

Bandura A. (1997). *Self-efficacy: The exercise of control.* New York: Freeman.

Bernard, J.M., & Goodyear, R.K. (2014). *Fundamentals of clinical supervision.* Boston: Merrill.

Campbell, J. (2001). *Thou art that.* Novato, CA: Joseph Campbell Foundation.

Crocket, K. (2004). Storying counselors: Producing professional selves in supervision. In D.A. Paré, & G. Larner (Eds.), *Collaborative practice in psychology and therapy* (pp. 171–182). New York: Haworth Press.

Erikson, E.H. (1968). *Identity, youth, and crisis.* New York: W.W. Norton.

Guiffrida, D.A. (2005). The emergence model: An alternative pedagogy for facilitating self-reflection and theoretical fit in counseling students. *Counselor Education and Supervision, 44,* 201–213.

Hackney, H., & Goodyear, R.K. (1984). Carl roger's client-centered approach to supervision. In R.F. Levant, & J.M. Shlien (Eds.), *Client-centered therapy and the person-centered approach: New directions in theory, research, and practice* (pp. 278–296). New York: Praeger.

Ivey, A.E., & Goncalves, O.F. (1988). Developmental therapy: Integrating developmental processes into the clinical practice. *Journal of Counseling & Development, 66*(9), 406–413.

Kegan, R. (1998). *In over our heads: The mental demands of modern life.* Cambridge, MA: Harvard University Press.

Kelly, G.A. (1955). *The psychology of personal constructs.* New York: W.W. Norton.

Kohlberg, L. (1969). Stage and sequence: The cognitive-developmental approach to socialization. In D.A. Goslin (Ed.), *The handbook of socialization theory and research* (pp. 347–480). Chicago: Rand McNally.

Krishnamurti, J. (1953) *Education and the significance of life.* New York: Harper & Row.

Lyddon, W.J., & Weill, R. (1997). Cognitive psychotherapy and postmodernism: Emerging themes and challenges. *Journal of Cognitive Psychotherapy, 11*(2), 75–90.

Mahoney, M.J. (1991). *Human change processes.* New York: Basic Books.

Mahoney, M.J. (1988). Constructive metatheory: Basic features and historical foundations. *International Journal of Personal Construct Psychology, 1*(1), 1–35.

Mahoney, M.J. (2004). What is constructivism and why is it growing? *Psychcritiques, 49*(3), 360–363.

Mahoney, M.J. (2006). *Constructive psychotherapy: Theory and practice.* New York: Guilford.

McAuliffe, G.J. (2011). Constructing counselor education. In G.J. McAuliffe & K.P. Eriksen (Eds.), *Handbook of counselor preparation: Constructivist, developmental, and experiential approaches* (pp. 3–12). Thousand Oaks, CA: Sage.

McAuliffe, G.J., & Eriksen, K.P. (1999). Toward a constructivist and developmental identity for the counseling profession: The context-phase-stage-style model. *Journal of Counseling & Development, 77*(3), 267–280.

McAuliffe, G.J., & Lovell, C.W. (2006). The influence of counselor epistemology on the helping interview: A qualitative study. *Journal of Counseling and Development, 8,* 308–317.

Mezirow, J. (1997). Transformative learning: Theory to practice. In P. Cranton (Ed.), *Transformative learning in action: Insights from practice* (pp. 5–13). San Francisco: Jossey-Bass.

Miller, J. (2001). Learning from a spiritual perspective. In E. O'Sullivan, A. Morelli, & M.A. O'Connor (Eds.), *Expanding the boundaries of transformative learning* (pp. 95–102). New York: Palgrave.

Neimeyer, G.J. (1995). The challenge of change. In R.A. Neimeyer & M.J. Mahoney (Eds.), *Constructivism in psychotherapy* (pp. 111–126). Washington, DC: American Psychological Association.

Neimeyer, R.A. (1995). Constructivist psychotherapies: Features, foundations, and future directions. In R.A. Neimeyer & M.J. Mahoney (Eds.), *Constructivism in psychotherapy* (pp. 11–38). Washington, DC: American Psychological Association.

Neimeyer, R.A. (2009). *Constructivist psychotherapy: Distinctive features.* New York: Routledge.

Neimeyer, R.A., & Mahoney, M.J., Eds. (1995). *Constructivism in psychotherapy.* Washington, DC: American Psychological Association.

Perry, W.G. (1998). *Forms of intellectual and ethical development in college years: A scheme.* San Francisco: Jossey Bass (original work published 1970).

Piaget, J. (1954). *The construction of reality in the child.* New York: Basic Books.

Schon, D.A. (1995). The new scholarship. *Change,* Nov/Dec, 27–34.

Skovholt, T.M., & Ronnestad, M.H. (1992). Themes in therapist and counselor development. *Journal of Counseling & Development, 70*(4), 505–515.

Steenbarger, B.N. (1991). All the world is not a stage: Emerging contextualist themes in counseling and development. *Journal of Counseling & Development, 70*(2), 288–296.

Stoltenberg, C.D., & McNeill, B.W. (2010). *IDM supervision: An integrative developmental model for supervising counselors and therapists* (3rd ed.). New York: Routledge.

von Glasersfeld, E. (1995). *Radical constructivism: A way of knowing and learning.* Studies in mathematics education series: 6. London: Falmer Press, Taylor & Francis.

Wilson, R.A. (1990). *Quantum psychology: How brain software programs you and your world.* Tempe, AZ: New Falcon Publications.

Wilson, R.A. (2005, April). *Robert Anton Wilson explains everything (or old Bob exposes his ignorance).* Retrieved July 24, 2013, from www.soundstrue.com/shop/Robert-Anton-Wilson-Explains-Everything/309.pd

2

INFLUENTIAL THEORIES OF PSYCHOTHERAPY

Although clinical supervision is a distinct intervention from psychotherapy, with its own research, models, and interventions, many models of supervision have derived from theories of psychotherapy. This is due, in part, to the overlap that exists between roles and functions of psychotherapy and clinical supervision. It is also due to the fact that models of clinical supervision were developed by psychotherapists, who began viewing the process of supervision through the same lenses through which they viewed psychotherapy (Bernard & Goodyear, 2014).

Like other models of clinical supervision, the constructive approach is heavily influenced by theories of psychotherapy. Consistent with Mahoney's (2006) constructive psychotherapy, constructive supervision integrates constructivist perspectives of human growth, change, and learning with several theories of psychotherapy to provide an integrative meta-theory for conceptualizing supervisee development and implementing interventions. As such, the approach is applicable to supervisors from any counseling orientation. Moreover, unlike many other models of supervision that are based upon theories of psychotherapy, this approach does not require that supervisees adhere to the same theoretical orientation as the supervisor.

I begin by describing the centrality of the core conditions of Person-Centered Therapy (Rogers, 1957) to the constructive approach to clinical supervision. Second, I describe how the principles of Self-Determination Theory (SDT; Deci & Ryan, 1991), a theory of motivation that has been increasingly applied to psychotherapy, can be implemented by supervisors to foster intrinsic motivation in supervisees. I then describe the ways in which mindfulness and mindfulness-based therapies can be integrated by both supervisors and supervisees to enhance the process of clinical supervision. I conclude by providing a description of several core principles of psychoanalytic therapy that can be used in clinical supervision. Taken together, these four theories of psychotherapy, which each address growth and change from varying perspectives, are integrated in a way that allows supervisors to facilitate supervisee development from a constructive perspective.

Person-Centered Therapy

Rogers' (1951) Person-Centered Therapy is one of the most researched and empirically supported theories of psychotherapy (Kirschenbaum, 2009). At the core of Rogers' approach is that clients have the potential to find their own meaningful answers in therapy if therapists provide the necessary conditions under which this can occur; these conditions include unconditional positive regard, empathic understanding, and congruence. Therapists who provide these conditions, according to Rogers, are able to form solid, trusting relationships with clients. The counselor/client relationship then becomes the foundation upon which the process of client change begins. Additionally, Rogers advocated that therapists use a non-directive approach that allowed clients to freely explore issues of meaning to them and to discover their own answers to problems. As I will detail below, Rogers' core conditions for forming relationships and his non-directive approach are also central to facilitating supervisee change from a constructive approach to supervision.

Relationship

As described in Chapter 1, constructivists believe that humans have an inherent need to form relationships with others and that much of the order we make of the world results from interpersonal relationships. Consistent with Rogers' approach to counseling, the quality of the relationship between the counselor and client is central to facilitating client growth and development from a constructivist perspective (Neimeyer, 1995). Mahoney (2006) has referred to the counselor/client relationship as an *anchor* in constructive psychotherapy in that it allows clients to tentatively explore unknown and often frightening places while maintaining a secure connection to someone who will prevent them from drifting too far into dangerous waters. In this same way, a constructive supervisor strives to form relationships with supervisees that allow them to tentatively and safely explore new ways of understanding and being with their clients.

The first core condition outlined by Rogers (1957) for facilitating therapeutic relationships is unconditional positive regard, which is when therapists demonstrate genuine acceptance of all client thoughts, feelings, and experiences. Through experiencing this deep acceptance, Rogers believed that people could drop their resistances and become open to explore failures, insecurities, and painful experiences without the fear of being judged harshly or losing the respect, concern, and care of the therapist. Rogers also asserted that clients failed to develop in healthy ways when their behaviors were geared primarily toward pleasing others, including the therapist.

Similarly, supervisor unconditional positive regard for the supervisee is central in facilitating the conditions necessary for change in constructive supervision.

Unconditional positive regard can be established in supervision when supervisors genuinely convey confidence in their supervisees' abilities to develop and grow as counselors, even in times in which they become frustrated or appear to struggle; to trust supervisees to select the focus of supervision, including identifying their own strengths, weaknesses, and goals for supervision; and to develop their own conceptualizations and interventions, even if they might be different than the conceptualizations of the supervisor. Constructive supervisors, therefore, convey to supervisees that they trust in them and accept them, even in times when they may be struggling or conducting therapy in a way that is different than the way the supervisor would have proceeded.

Unconditional positive regard does not, however, mean that supervisors must uncritically accept and agree with all supervisee ideas and statements. Rather, strong positive regard for supervisees can be established when supervisors regularly pose questions to supervisees that help them critically reflect upon their thoughts, feelings, and behaviors in counseling and in supervision. Demonstrating positive regard while facilitating reflective thinking may, at first glance, seem contradictory; however, reflective questioning, when asked empathically and consistently (including times when supervisors internally "agree" with supervisees), can, in many ways, facilitate an even deeper sense of positive regard for supervisees than simply agreeing with them all of the time. In other words, by asking supervisees to regularly consider *how* they know what they know, supervisors can convey that they trust supervisees enough to carefully question all of their positions without challenging their legitimacy as experts regarding their clients. This inquiry-based approach of facilitating critical self-reflection is highly consistent with the *consultant* role of supervision (Bernard, 1979) and will be described in much more detail in Chapter 3.

The second core condition outlined by Rogers (1957) is that counselors must have strong empathy for the struggles of their clients. In this same way, supervisor empathy for the developmental challenges of their supervisees is of critical importance in facilitating change in supervisees. It can, however, be difficult sometimes for supervisors to empathize with supervisees in the same way they do with clients. Lack of empathy can be particularly problematic when supervision is viewed by the supervisor's employer as an ancillary activity done in addition to or at the expense of their *real* work. For this reason, it is critically important that supervision be valued by institutions and conducted by those who enjoy this work and appreciate the importance of quality, ongoing supervision to the success of every practitioner.

Lack of empathy for supervisees can also result when supervisors lose sight of the developmental challenges that are inherent in the psychotherapy process. One way in which supervisors can develop empathy for their supervisees is to become familiar with the models of counselor development described in Chapter 1. Familiarity with these models can help normalize what can sometimes feel like abnormal behaviors and reactions by supervisees, including focusing more on themselves than on clients, hesitancy in exploring strong client emotions, allowing countertransference issues to impact sessions, or eschewing established theories in attempts to be more creative in their work. As described in Chapter 1, an understanding of counselor development can allow supervisors to be more patient and understanding when their supervisees engage in what can otherwise be perceived as problematic behavior.

Additionally, reading about and discussing models of counselor development can assist supervisors in remembering their own experiences in supervision, thus encouraging them to connect with the experiences of their supervisees. It is amazing to me how much counselors remember about their supervisors and their experiences in supervision, some even being able to vividly recall interactions that occurred with their supervisors twenty or thirty years ago. Often these memories reflect the attitudes they felt the supervisors had toward them (i.e., they liked or disliked me), which underscores the centrality of both positive regard and empathy in establishing relationships that support change.

The third core condition outlined by Rogers (1957) for facilitating therapeutic relationships is congruence, which is when a person's behavior is consistent with their current experience and their ideal self, or who they would like to be. This core condition is also sometimes referred to as *genuineness*. Rogers astutely observed that it was not enough for the therapist to simply demonstrate empathy and positive regard for clients; for therapy to be effective, the therapist had to genuinely feel empathy and positive regard as well. In this sense, Rogers (1980) asserted that Client-Centered Therapy was more than just a set of techniques, it was actually a way of being.

Like person-centered therapists, constructive supervisors must be genuine in their positive regard and empathy for supervisees. Moreover, constructive supervisors need not only to understand, but also to trust in the constructivist theories of human development, change, and learning described in Chapter 1 for constructive supervision to be effective. Supervisors cannot effectively allow supervisees to discover their own answers, for example, if they believe that, deep down, one counseling approach is better or more effective than others. Supervisors cannot effectively assist supervisees in exploring strengths and limitations of their predisposed notions of helping if they also assume that these predisposed notions are irrelevant to the current experience. And supervisors cannot effectively help supervisees normalize and embrace mistakes and anxiety if they themselves are highly fearful of making mistakes or are feeling extremely anxious about the performance of the supervisee or their work as a supervisor. Constructive supervisors, therefore, must genuinely believe in, or at least be open to considering and experimenting with, constructivist principles of learning and development in order to effectively conduct supervision using this approach.

Non-Directiveness

In addition to highlighting the centrality of the counselor/client relationship to the process of psychotherapy, Rogers (1951) also advocated that counselors use a non-directive approach that allows clients the flexibility to discuss the issues of meaning to them. The non-directive approach, to varying degrees, is also emphasized in constructivist approaches to psychotherapy. Mahoney (2006) used the term *teleonomic* to describe the process by which a constructive psychotherapist allows the client to lead a session. Most traditional forms of psychotherapy, according to Mahoney, are based on a teleological pattern, which he defined as "movement with directionality determined by an explicit destination" (p. 390). A teleological approach to supervision would begin with supervisors establishing specific goals for their supervisees, which can include things like learning to ask more open-ended questions, becoming comfortable with silence, understanding how to conceptualize and intervene from a particular theoretical approach, or becoming more culturally competent. These goals, all of which are very important goals of counselor development, then become learning outcomes to be assessed at the end of the experience.

Constructivists, while paying attention to the teleological position, operate more from a teleonomic position, which Mahoney defined as "movement that reflects directionality that is not defined by an explicit destination" (p. 390). From a teleonomic position, supervisors encourage supervisees to direct the sessions, including allowing them to determine goals for the sessions, to assist supervisees in developing their own answers to their questions, and encouraging them to self-evaluate on their progress. This is not to say that supervisors must always refrain from providing direction, advice, or evaluation; rather, they direct sparingly and only when absolutely necessary.

To illustrate the effectiveness of the teleonomic position in counseling, Mahoney offered the example of the counselor and client as travel companions. This same metaphor can be useful to conceptualize the teleonomic position that is central to constructive supervision. Modernist supervisors often assume the role of *travel agents*: well-traveled themselves, they seek to provide roadmaps to help guide supervisees in their travels; take a certain road, avoid others, often even selling them on the destination itself. The constructive supervisor would not assume a travel agent role, but rather, would serve as a *travel partner* who joins the supervisee in the process of traveling. This type of supervisor empowers supervisees to take the lead in deciding where to go; how fast to move; and, in some cases, even the final destination.

Inherent in the non-directive approach is the fundamental tenet that supervisees have within themselves the capacity to discover their own answers. Moreover, consistent with constructive approaches to learning, the approach espouses that meaningful answers can only be discovered from within supervisees through a process of critical self-reflection. Consistent with Rogers' Person-Centered Approach, the main goal of constructive supervision is for supervisors not to impart knowledge to their supervisees through didactic instruction or advice, but to provide the necessary conditions under which supervisees can discover their own answers.

The power of the relationship and the non-directive approach outlined by Rogers forms the foundation of the constructive approach to supervision. It is important to note, however, that the person-centered approach (PCA) has been formally applied to the process of supervision (Patterson, 1997), and that the constructive approach outlined in this book deviates from the PCA to clinical supervision in several ways. In particular, Patterson insisted that the supervisor and supervisee share the same theoretical orientation for supervision to be successful. In fact, Patterson suggested that the supervisor, ideally, had served as a prior instructor of counseling theories to the supervisee so that the supervisee began supervision with a clear understanding of the preferences and expectations of the supervisor. Additionally, both Patterson and Rogers placed strong emphases on teaching supervisees to think in the same ways as their supervisors. Rogers, in particular, frequently provided supervisees with suggestions and ideas on how he would have handled certain situations, which he believed would "stimulate the imagination" of supervisees (Hackney & Goodyear, 1984, p. 289).

While the constructive approach outlined in this book is clearly rooted in the core ingredients outlined by Rogers' PCA to counseling, it deviates in some important ways from the PCA to clinical supervision as outlined by Rogers and Patterson by (1) relying less on modeling and suggestions from the supervisor and (2) integrating several other theories of psychotherapy to facilitate self-reflection and change. In the next section I will delineate how the principles of SDT, a theory of intrinsic motivation, can be utilized by supervisors to enhance supervisor/supervisee relationships; and to understand when and how to provide advice, direction, and compliments during supervision in ways that enhance supervisee autonomy and intrinsic motivation to learn and grow.

Self-Determination Theory (SDT)

Client motivation to change is widely recognized as one of the most important predictors of success in counseling and psychotherapy; change and growth require movement and clients must be motivated for movement to occur (Ryan, Lynch, Vansteenkiste, & Deci, 2011). This relationship between movement, growth, and change is also central to the process of clinical supervision. From this perspective, clinical supervision can be conceptualized, in part, as a process in which supervisors provide conditions under which supervisees become motivated to change and grow. But how do people assist others in becoming motivated to make changes that allow them to develop and grow? This is a question that clinical and social psychologists have explored for decades and a rich base of motivational research now exists to help us understand these dynamic processes. This motivational research is useful in understanding the conditions that facilitate supervisee motivation to change in clinical supervision.

For much of the 20th century, it was believed that motivation was driven by innate biological forces such as hunger, thirst, and sex (Freud, 1949); or extrinsic rewards and punishments (Skinner, 1953; Watson, 1913). Neither of these views, however, explained motivation in the absence of biological or behavioral rewards.

To explain this, researchers theorized that motivation could also be derived purely from satisfaction inherent in the activity itself, which psychologists have labeled *intrinsic motivation* (White, 1959; Woodworth, 1921).

One of the first studies to highlight the power of intrinsic motivation and the limitations of extrinsic motivation was conducted by Edward Deci (1972). Deci asked two groups of college students to participate in a puzzle activity: one group received $1 each time they completed a puzzle (which was worth a lot more at that time) and the other group received no reward for completing the puzzle. After participating in the puzzle for several minutes, the researcher would leave the room for exactly eight minutes (supposedly to take care of paperwork), leaving the student alone in the room with the puzzle. The experimenter then observed what the students did during this free time. Deci found that students who were not monetarily rewarded for completing the puzzle were far more likely to continue playing with the puzzle during the free time than students who were paid for playing with the puzzle. Deci concluded that the extrinsic reward (the payment) led students to lose interest in the activity once the rewards ceased and, as a result, thwarted their intrinsic motivation for completing the task.

Since this initial study, Deci, along with Richard Ryan and numerous other colleagues, have conducted hundreds of additional studies examining the effects of extrinsic and intrinsic motivation on human behavior. This research has led to the development of a sophisticated theory of motivation, called Self-Determination Theory (SDT; Deci & Ryan, 1991), which is now the most referenced and empirically supported theory of human motivation. According to SDT, there are three primary psychological needs (or nutriments) that, when satisfied, foster intrinsic motivation: (a) autonomy, which occurs when people choose to become engaged in an activity because the subject and activities are closely aligned with their interests and values; (b) competence, which is the need to test and challenge one's abilities; and (c) relatedness, which is the need to establish close, secure relationships with others. SDT asserts that these three psychological needs are innate to all humans and that they are essential to psychological health and well-being.

SDT also recognizes that extrinsic motivation, while effective in motivating people toward short-term behaviors, is often less successful in sustaining meaningful, long-term motivation. Further, SDT conceptualizes different forms of extrinsic motivation that are based upon their positioning along a continuum of relative autonomy. The least self-determined form of motivation (i.e., farthest away from intrinsic motivation) is *external regulation*, which occurs when people are motivated purely by rewards and punishments. Next along the continuum is *introjected regulation*, which occurs when people who are motivated by rewards and punishments begin to associate self-worth and esteem through the achievement of awards or the avoidance of punishment. The form of extrinsic motivation closest on the continuum to intrinsic motivation *identified regulation*, which occurs when the externalized pressure becomes internalized by the individual. These extrinsic forms of motivation, in addition to being less likely than intrinsic motivation to provide lasting behavior change, are also negatively correlated with psychological health and well-being when compared to motivation derived from intrinsic motivation. In other words, people tend to be happier and healthier in environments that provide autonomy, competence, and relatedness. The absence of either intrinsic or extrinsic motivation results in what Deci and Ryan refer to as *amotivation*.

SDT has been applied and empirically supported in a wide variety of settings, including education, business, athletics, parenting, and healthcare, and the theory is increasingly being applied in a wide array of counseling and psychotherapeutic interventions (Ryan et al., 2011). Additionally, research conducted in a number of countries outside of the United States suggests strong cross-cultural support for the theory (e.g. Chirkov, Ryan, Kim, and Kaplan, 2003;Vansteenkiste, Zhou, Lens, and Soenens, 2005). While a review of the literature failed to reveal any studies that have examined the efficacy of SDT when applied to clinical supervision, the strong empirical support for the theory in related areas, including education (Reeve, Deci, & Ryan, 2004) and business/organizational supervision (Stone, Deci, & Ryan, 2009), suggest strong applicability to clinical supervision. The principles of SDT, therefore, provide a useful lens for understanding how supervisors can facilitate supervisee motivation to change.

Fostering Intrinsic Motivation Through Autonomy-Supportive Supervision

As detailed in Chapter 1, counselor development research clearly indicates that counselors, particularly early in their careers, experience high levels of motivation. SDT provides a way in which supervisors can tap into this natural motivation and avoid supervision strategies that can thwart counselors' natural motivation. According to the principles of SDT, supervisors seeking to foster intrinsic motivation in their supervisees must provide an *autonomy supportive* environment, which revolves around providing conditions that foster the three basic needs of autonomy, competence, and relatedness.

The core of autonomy-supportive supervision is that supervisors provide supervisees with a sense of autonomy. Consistent with Person-Centered Therapy, this is demonstrated most effectively when supervisees are encouraged to make decisions and act based upon their own free will rather than being pressured to act by the supervisor. Supervisors who provide autonomy for their supervisees encourage them to find their own voice as therapists and choose their own paths to follow with clients. They provide opportunities for supervisees to critically reflect on their work and to develop their own ideas. Rather than coercing supervisees to act in certain ways through expert and evaluative authority, autonomy supportive supervisors encourage supervisees to take ownership of the counseling process, including formulating their own case conceptualizations and interventions.

While SDT acknowledges the saliency of supervisors providing opportunities for supervisees to develop their own answers in supervision, the theory also acknowledges that autonomy is "not inconsistent with following external guidance or even commands, provided the person receiving them self-endorses or authentically accepts their legitimacy and concurs" (Ryan et al., 2011, p. 232). From an SDT perspective, some advice and direction is acceptable as long as these directives are used sparingly and the supervisees accept them as relevant options to consider from a legitimate source. SDT asserts that advice is most effective when it is provided with a meaningful rationale, without force or coercion, and in a way that provides supervisees with choices about how and when to follow it. Space should also be provided for the supervisee to openly acknowledge any resistance they may have to the advice or negative feelings that may result from this more supervisor-directed form of supervision.

Consistent with Rogers' (1957) idea of non-directiveness, another autonomy supportive measure that supervisors can take in clinical supervision is to allow supervisees to have primary control of the agenda for the supervision session. This can include encouraging them to think ahead of time about this agenda and to come prepared with the issues they would like to discuss. One fairly common approach that fails to consider supervisee autonomy is when supervisors view a supervisee's counseling session ahead of time (either in person or on a tape) and then arrive at the supervision ready to critique the supervisee's performance. Despite the supervisor's best attempt to provide useful, sensitive feedback, this process is often, from my experience, met with anxiety and resistance from supervisees. The principles outlined in SDT suggest that watching or listening to counseling tapes ahead of time could limit supervisee autonomy by placing control of the session squarely in the hands of the supervisor. In fact, from an SDT perspective, this might be considered a form of surveillance, which is a technique that has been extensively proven to greatly reduce intrinsic motivation (Reeve et al., 2004; Stone et al., 2009). A more autonomy-supportive way of providing supervision places control of the session, including choosing which sections of sessions to review or discuss, primarily in the hands of the supervisees.

Another more fundamental aspect of supervisee autonomy revolves around the supervisee's ability to freely choose counseling as a profession or field of study. Research in the field of higher education indicates that students who freely choose their own fields of study are much more successful in college than those who feel coerced to choose a certain major (Guiffrida, Lynch, Wall, & Able, 2013). Presumably, supervisees will have entered the field of counseling based on their own free choice to pursue their intrinsic interests in helping others. Likewise, those supervisees who are veterans in the field have likely remained in the profession and, in some cases, sought supervision (it is not always required or provided in every setting) because of an intrinsic interest in improving. The reality is, however, that this assumption is not true in all cases. Some new supervisees may have been compelled by others to study counseling. These supervisees often experience a strong sense of amotivation once they begin their clinical experiences. Likewise, there are some veteran counselors who have experienced burnout and no longer gain the same sense of pride or satisfaction from their jobs they once did. While many counselors who lose their motivation often leave the field to follow other intrinsic interests, some feel trapped to remain in the field because they perceive themselves as lacking other viable options. These amotivated counselors often struggle in supervision, even when supervisors provide autonomy-supportive conditions. Supervisors need to carefully decide upon interventions with amotivated supervisees, which can range from attempting to foster intrinsic motivation, to openly discussing with them their apparent lack of motivation and potential poor fit for the field.

The second core condition or psychological need that must be fostered in supervision for supervisees to experience intrinsic motivation is *competence*. Competence, from an SDT perspective, often evolves as a result of the autonomy that supervisees experience. In other words, the sense of trust supervisees experience from supervisors who provide them with the autonomy to develop their own case conceptualizations and interventions can also lead to increases in supervisee competence. Likewise, competence will also increase as supervisees experience success in implementing their autonomously chosen approaches with their clients. Supervisors should also caution supervisees about the problems inherent in assessing their competence based on relatively short-term, day-to-day client outcomes, which is common among new counselors. Supervisees should be encouraged to take a longitudinal view of their clients' progress and their own development as counselors.

Related to the issue of competence is the proper use of supervisor praise for supervisees. From an SDT perspective, praise is viewed as a "double-edged sword" (Ryan et al., 2011, p. 231) with regard to its effect on competence motivation and, as a result, needs to be used carefully. Ryan et al. assert that praise can promote autonomy when people are praised for process issues, including taking their own initiative, thinking critically about their work, and being creative in therapy and in supervision. SDT research also suggests, however, that praise can thwart intrinsic motivation when used to motivate supervisees toward a specific, supervisor-imposed outcome and can also make supervisees less autonomous as they become motivated to act in order to receive praise. Therefore, rather than complimenting supervisee performance or specific skills (e.g., "That was excellent how you developed rapport with the client"), it can be more meaningful to compliment the process that supervisees engage in during supervision. Examples of such compliments can include, "I really like the way you are thinking about this" or "I can tell this is difficult for you but you're working hard and coming up with answers for yourself, which is the most meaningful way to learn." These types of process-oriented compliments convey to supervisees the trust the supervisor has in them to develop their own answers while also normalizing the intense struggles they may experience as they embark on the process of self-discovery.

The third condition necessary to foster intrinsic motivation in supervisees is *relatedness*. As noted earlier, the supervisor/supervisee relationship is central to the process of constructive supervision. Supervisees must experience a strong sense of relatedness to the supervisor to engage meaningfully in supervision. Consistent with the Person-Centered Approach, relationships, from an SDT perspective, form best when supervisors provide unconditional positive regard, empathy, and congruence. These core conditions have already been discussed in the previous person-centered section; however, given the centrality of the supervisor/supervisee relationship to the process of clinical supervision, it is useful to also consider additional theories that have illuminated ways in which meaningful relationships can be facilitated in clinical settings. One particularly useful approach for facilitating empathy and the ability to be fully present with others is mindfulness and Mindfulness-Based Therapy. As I will detail in the next section, integrating mindfulness into the process of supervision can not only assist supervisors in facilitating meaningful relationships with supervisees, but can also teach supervisees to embrace and work with the anxiety that is inherent to clinical supervision.

Mindfulness-Based Therapy

Mindfulness is becoming increasingly popular among counselors and psychotherapists. A recent search of the database PsycINFO® revealed more than 1,400 articles with the term *mindfulness* in the title. It has been formally integrated into several popular, contemporary theories of psychotherapy, including Dialectical Behavior Therapy (DBT; Linehan, Cochran & Kehrer, 2001), Mindfulness-Based Cognitive Therapy (MBCT; Segal, Williams, & Teasdale, 2002), and Acceptance and Commitment Therapy (ACT; Hayes, Luoma, Bond, Masuda, & Lillis, 2006; Hayes, Strosahl, & Wilson, 1999) and is utilized by many other clinicians who identify as integrative or eclectic in their approaches. The *Psychotherapy Networker*, an interdisciplinary psychotherapy publication, found that over 41 percent of the 2,600 therapists who completed their survey reported integrating some form of mindfulness into their therapy practice (Siegal, 2011). Yet despite the increased attention of mindfulness in the field, it is still a relatively new approach that is far less recognizable and understood by counselors and psychotherapists than the person-centered and motivational approaches I discussed at the beginning of the chapter. Below I provide a brief definition of mindfulness and then describe some of the ways in which mindfulness can be integrated into the process of clinical supervision.

What Is Mindfulness?

The term *mindfulness* comes from the teachings of the Buddha over 2,500 years ago. Consistent with Buddhist traditions of teaching, which highlight the limitations of language in conveying complex phenomena (if you can describe it, that's not it!), I will begin by defining mindfulness by first describing what it is not. First, mindfulness is not a religion. While it is associated with Buddhism, it is practiced by people from all faiths for religious and other purposes. Some have even asserted that mindfulness practices date back thousands of years before the Buddha's time, with roots in ancient yogic practices (Miller, Fletcher, & Kabat-Zinn, 1995). Second, mindfulness is not a technique. While techniques, most notably, various forms of meditation, can be used to help facilitate mindful states, mindfulness is a state of being rather than a technique. Third, mindfulness is not focused on relaxation or stress reduction. While these states can and often do result from mindful practice, mindfulness embraces all emotional states, including anxiety and anger. Fourth, mindfulness is not about escaping; in fact, it is the opposite—it's about learning to be exactly where you are.

So what is mindfulness? Jon Kabat-Zinn (1994), the person most often credited with bringing mindfulness to contemporary Western healing practices, defines mindfulness as "paying attention in a particular way: on purpose, in the present moment, and nonjudgmentally" (p. 4). To understand this concept, it is useful to examine each aspect of this definition more carefully. The first and most important element stresses the need to *pay attention*. From a mindful perspective, most people suffer from a widespread form of attention deficit disorder in the sense that we tend to pay close attention to the endless stream of thoughts within our head at the expense of paying attention to our immediate surroundings or internal sensations. Mindfulness, at its core, involves purposefully learning to pay attention in a new way.

The next part of the definition provides insight into where our attention must focus to be mindful, which begins by focusing *in the present moment*. When people examine the actual content of their thoughts, it becomes apparent that most of our time and energy is spent needlessly thinking about the past or planning and worrying about the future. As Kabat-Zinn and numerous other mindfulness teachers have pointed out, the present moment is the only moment we are alive in, yet it occupies very little of our awareness. Even as you are reading this book, it is likely that your thoughts have drifted from time to time to reliving moments from the past (e.g., "I can't believe I said something so stupid in that meeting") and planning for the future (e.g., "What do I have to do after I finish this?"). This is not to say that all forms of remembering or planning are inherently bad. It can be useful to reflect on past experiences or spend time planning future courses of action. Mindfulness, however, helps us realize that most of this self-talk is not only unnecessary, but also can actually be incredibly harmful by preventing us from experiencing the fullness and richness of the present moment.

Kabat-Zinn's definition of mindfulness also stresses the importance of being *non-judgmental*. Again, when examining the content of our thoughts, it is amazing to see just how much of our time is spent making judgments about things, people, events, etc. before or instead of fully experiencing them. When I present on this topic, I often make jokes about the judgments attendees are making about me as I begin the talk: "I hope he doesn't talk long," "Why is he dressed that way?" "I wonder if he shaved his head because he is going bald?" These comments usually draw laughter from the folks in attendance and my sense is that the biggest laughs come from people who have actually made these judgments about me and the presentation prior to my pointing this out. I am able to point out things that some of them are thinking because I too am guilty of making judgments about speakers when attending a presentation!

A natural consequence to our nearly constant state of judging is that we develop preferred states of being and we try continuously to avoid states we perceive as painful or uncomfortable. While it may be easy to avoid some painful states, like learning not to touch a hot stove, many other painful aspects of life are unavoidable. As a result, it can be harmful to focus one's time and energy on the avoidance of pain. Mindfulness teaches us to accept all experiences, feelings, and even thoughts (no matter how painful and unpleasant) without resistance. While we cannot avoid pain, we can recognize the tendency of our thought patterns to turn pain into suffering. Examples of thoughts that transform pain into suffering include the following: "Why me?" "I (or someone else) do not deserve this," or "How long must this go on?" Without thought, pain is just pain; but thoughts, specifically, the inability to accept and experience the pain, are what transforms pain to suffering.

Unlike Cognitive Behavioral Therapy, mindfulness does not encourage us to dispute or fight these injurious thoughts, but seeks to help us change our *relationship* to our thoughts. Instead of reacting needlessly to our endless stream of thoughts, mindfulness teaches us to non-judgmentally observe our thoughts. Moreover, mindfulness teaches us to transform our identity from that of the *thinker* (I am my thoughts) to that of the *observer* of this process (I am the one watching my thoughts). Through this practice of de-identifying with thought, we are better able to recognize our thoughts as perspectives (often faulty ones) rather than ontological reality.

The combination of failing to be present while continually making judgments can cause us to miss out on much of our lives. This phenomenon was illustrated beautifully in the movie *Click* starring Adam Sandler. In the movie, Sandler's character was going through a difficult time in his life: he was working long hours with the promise of a big promotion while also juggling a busy family life. He is preoccupied with thoughts about how awful his current life situation is but believes that it will all be better soon if he can just get through this one difficult time. He soon discovers a magical remote control that allows him to fast forward through parts of his life and he begins to take full advantage of the fast forward button anytime he experiences something painful or difficult that he would prefer to speed through. While in fast forward mode, he performs as if he is on "autopilot," monotonously plugging through the difficulties without being present. Eventually, he loses the ability to handle even the smallest amount of discomfort and the remote begins automatically fast-forwarding his life anytime it perceives difficulties. Soon, the character becomes an old man on his death-bed and he is left wondering how he allowed his life to pass him by so quickly without experiencing any of it. He begs for another chance and, magically, he is transformed back to his former, pre-remote control state, with a new appreciation for living life fully present.

I have found this story relevant to the way many of us live our lives; spending countless hours fretting about the past, planning for the future, and making constant judgments about ourselves and the world around us. How often have we thought, "If I can just get through . . . then everything will be fine." Unfortunately, the day we are waiting for often never arrives and even if it does, our minds are so programmed to look to the future and judge that we are unable to be fully present enough to enjoy the accomplishments or good times we have sacrificed so much for to attain.

An example I often give to illustrate this point is the college student experience, which can sometimes feel like a very difficult time of life. College students work hard, have few financial resources, and a relatively low social status. As a result, some students spend enormous amounts of time dreaming of the time when they finish and can finally live the life they want. It is often not until we graduate that we realize just how amazing the college experience was, free from all the responsibility that comes with entrance into the real world. How much more would we have enjoyed our college experiences had we truly realized just how special a time it was? Mindfulness teaches us that while it is fine to have goals and dreams for the future, all moments, even those that seem difficult at the time, are special and must be fully experienced rather than sped through on autopilot.

Over the past thirty years, there has been an explosion of research supporting the efficacy of mindfulness-based interventions for a wide variety of issues ranging from physical health (e.g., psoriasis, chronic pain, migraine headaches) to severe psychological issues (e.g., depression, anxiety, substance abuse, eating disorders; see Chambers, Gullone, & Allen, 2009 for a review). Mindfulness-based interventions have even been found to improve academic outcomes in students of all ages, from those in elementary school (Hart, 2004) to college students (Hall, 1999). Additionally, several studies (Christopher & Maris, 2010; Schure, Christopher, & Christopher, 2008; Rothaupt & Morgan, 2007; Ryback & Russell-Chapin, 1998) have examined the effects of mindfulness training with graduate students from various counseling and psychotherapy programs and have concluded that mindfulness training helped students improve in a number of important outcomes, including listening more attentively to clients, feeling more relaxed when dealing with difficult client issues and emotions, and being more accepting of feedback from professors and supervisors. Perhaps most interesting is a study by Grepmair, Mitterlehner, Loew, Bachler, Rother, and Nickel (2007), which found that counselors who received mindfulness training had better client outcomes when compared with those counselors who did not receive mindfulness training, even though their clients did not know they received such training. While a thorough review of the mindfulness research is beyond the scope of this book, it is clear from the literature that this relatively simple approach has yielded positive outcomes in a number of areas that are relevant to counseling and psychotherapy practice, training, and supervision.

Mindful Clinical Supervision

The most foundational application of mindfulness in supervision is for supervisors themselves to be mindful during supervision. As described throughout this book thus far, the supervisor/supervisee relationship is central to the constructive approach to supervision. Supervisors who establish the core conditions outlined by Rogers (unconditional positive regard, empathy, and congruence) with their supervisees are likely to establish the types of trusting and secure relationships that are necessary for meaningful supervision to occur. These core conditions are not techniques to be mastered by supervisors; rather, they are ways of being with the supervisee. In addition to the exercises I described earlier for facilitating empathy (e.g., remembering one's own experience in supervision), mindfulness practice can allow supervisors to be fully present during supervision by helping them focus on each moment-to-moment interaction. Mindfulness also helps supervisors be more aware of their own thoughts and emotional reactions during supervision, including needs to help/protect supervisees or clients or to demonstrate competence. Rather than unconsciously reacting to these thoughts, mindful supervisors will be more likely to openly explore these reactions without judging themselves.

Another way in which mindfulness can be integrated into the supervision session is for supervisors to teach mindfulness to their supervisees. In fact, qualitative research suggests that supervisees who learn mindfulness are "more open, aware, self-accepting, and less defensive in supervision" (Christopher & Maris, 2010, p. 123), all of which are crucial to effective supervision, regardless of supervisor orientation. Supervisors using mindfulness with supervisees can begin by teaching them about the tendencies of the human mind to become preoccupied with thinking about the past, planning for the future, and labeling and making judgments about our everyday experiences. Supervisors should stress, in particular, how these tendencies can thwart the supervision process by making them overly nervous, self-conscious, and unable to effectively observe and reflect upon their own work. Supervisees who are not familiar with mindfulness can also be referred to literature that clearly describes mindfulness, which can include Kabat-Zinn (1994), Brown and Ryan (2003), and Brown, Marquis, and Guiffrida (2013).

For some supervisees, learning about and adopting the basic mindfulness philosophy may be all that is needed for supervisees to be more fully present and self-aware during the counseling and supervision sessions. Some supervisees, however, may seek additional training and experience in becoming more mindful in their counseling and supervision sessions. In these cases, supervisors may choose to teach supervisees some basic mindfulness-based exercises to help them learn to be more fully present. The most fundamental of these activities is basic mindfulness meditation, which is also referred to as *vipassana* meditation. Meditation is a word that has many different meanings and can involve a wide array of complex and esoteric processes; the core of all meditation, however, is most simply understood as attention training. For those who are interested in learning about how basic attention training activities can be integrated into clinical supervision, I have included descriptions of several basic mindfulness-based activities in Chapter 5.

While the idea of being fully present is often one that is congruent with many supervisors' perceptions of effective supervision, the more difficult aspect of mindful supervision for some supervisors to grasp is the idea of being *non-judgmental*. Supervision, after all, is *evaluative* and requires, therefore, that supervisors make judgments about their supervisees. Yet this process of being judgmental is often the aspect that can cause the most difficulty in the supervisor/supervisee relationship and the most angst on the part of both supervisor and supervisee. Mindfulness can provide a way of reframing this important but potentially disruptive aspect of clinical supervision so that supervisees learn to accept and even embrace all types of feedback and to critically self-reflect upon of their work.

One of the most important ways for supervisors to foster a more open, less judgmental setting in supervision is through the language that is used in the supervision session. Supervisors operating from more traditional, behaviorist approaches frequently make judgmental statements about the work of their supervisees, stating that they liked certain elements of the work, disliked other things the supervisees did, even using words like "good" or "bad" to describe elements of their approach or thinking. Likewise, supervisees also tend to make frequent judgments about themselves when presenting their work. A common example of such judgmental language from a supervisee is the following: "Oh, I'm so embarrassed and frustrated about this session. It was *terrible*." A supervisor operating from a more traditional, behaviorist approach might respond by trying to make the supervisee feel better by saying something like, "Oh, it wasn't so bad what you did." The supervisor might even try to point out some good in the interaction to make them feel more efficacious. This affirming statement is typically followed by the more traditional teaching statements about the negative aspects of the interaction, often stated very nicely, followed by suggestions about how the supervisee should do it differently next time. This approach, from my experience as someone who used to do it, often serves to make the supervisee either incredibly anxious or defensive, neither of which allows them to effectively hear the critique in a way in which they can learn.

A constructive supervisor will, instead, attempt to refrain from using judgmental or evaluative language, like "good" or "bad," as much as possible when describing the work of the supervisee and they encourage the same from their supervisees when describing their work. A supervisor acting from a more mindful-based, constructive perspective would encourage supervisees to reframe their statements in a way that eliminates the judgments and is more descriptive. For example, the supervisor may reply to the initial statement by the supervisee by stating, "It sounds like you are really frustrated with what happened in your last session, but, rather than saying it was good or bad, try restating this situation by being descriptive about what happened." To stick with the earlier example, the supervisee might follow-up by saying, "It just seemed really bad when I gave so much of my own opinion to the supervisee." A mindful, constructive response from the supervisor would encourage the supervisee to again eliminate the judgment and be more descriptive, "When you gave your own perspective, what happened for the client and what did it do to the flow of the session?" In this case, the supervisee might then respond by stating, "When I interrupted the client and began providing my own perspective to her, she became much quieter and less engaged in the session."

Once the judgmental statements are removed, it can become much easier for the supervisee to explain what happened and to understand how her actions may have affected the direction or context of the session. It might be fair, for example, for the supervisee to conclude that providing the client with her own opinion on the client's problem, in this case, may have interfered with the flow of the session and may have even damaged the counselor/client relationship. This more detailed description of what happened is much different than simply stating that what the supervisee did was *bad*. Supervisors can then provide a series of follow-up questions that encourage the supervisee to think critically about how her approach impacted the dynamics of the session, even asking her what she might have done differently if she had the opportunity to do it again. With the judgmental language removed, supervisees are often much more open to further exploration regarding the content of the session and even to explore deeper or hidden aspects that may have led them to choose this less preferable course of action. In this way, supervisees learn to critically self-reflect upon their work in meaningful ways while reducing the debilitating judgmental language that can cause them to rigidify rather than explore.

In my experience, most supervisees, even those who are not open to participating in mindfulness meditation activities, describe the mindful approach to supervision as extremely helpful in lessening their anxiety about supervision and helping them think more deeply and creatively about their counseling practice. Some supervisees find the approach so beneficial that they express an interest in learning to teach the process to their clients as a therapeutic intervention. In addition to continually practicing the approach during supervision, supervisors seeking to teach students how to effectively implement mindfulness into their counseling practice can also provide students with recommendations for literature that clearly explain the implementation of mindfulness in psychotherapy. Additionally, supervisors and supervisees for whom mindfulness resonates strongly may decide to implement additional mindfulness training activities into the supervision session, which, in addition to mindfulness-based meditation, can include activities that incorporate lovingkindness/compassion and mindful eating. Readers are referred to Chapter 4 for detailed descriptions of how these activities can be integrated into the clinical supervision session.

Psychoanalytic Therapy

As outlined in Chapter 1, a constructive approach to supervision involves a deep understanding of human change processes, which includes not only understanding conditions that facilitate meaningful growth and change in supervisees, but also recognizing factors that inhibit change processes. Constructivists view resistance to change as a natural manifestation of self-preservation during times of change that are perceived as threatening. Mahoney's constructivist model of change (2006), in particular, recognizes that people often inherently resist some necessary forms of change through the use of various defense mechanisms.

While most theories of counseling and supervision address issues of resistance among clients and supervisees, the most profound understandings of resistance to change derive from the work of Freud (1949) and his theory of psychoanalysis. At the core of Freud's theory lies the unconscious, which is a part of the human mind that operates below the level of conscious thought. According to Freud, the unconscious can impact and even direct human behavior through the use of defense mechanisms that distort reality to protect the ego from experiencing thoughts, feelings, or events that it believes to be too disturbing. While Freud believed defense mechanisms were normal and could even help people adapt to disturbing situations, he also asserted that they could lead to emotional and physical problems when relied on extensively. As a result, one main goal of Psychoanalytic Therapy is to assist clients in becoming aware of their unconscious minds and to recognize the defense mechanisms they use to protect themselves from experiencing reality. Through the use of techniques such as free association, dream analysis, interpretation, and analysis of resistance and transference, psychoanalytic therapists seek to help clients make the unconscious conscious. Additionally, they assist clients in recognizing the events, often from childhood, that contributed to the formation of their problematic, defensive posturing.

Freud's theory regarding the unconscious is central in understanding the ways in which resistance and supervisee defense mechanisms can manifest during supervision. There are, however, notable differences between the ways in which a traditional psychoanalyst would address resistance in supervision and the ways in which constructive supervisors approach supervisee resistance. Rather than attempting to interpret or battle unconscious defense mechanisms, constructive supervisors seek to join supervisees in identifying and developing their own idiographic understandings of their resistances. Based on constructivist principles of reality, supervisees are viewed as possessing expertise into their own experiences, while supervisors are viewed as partners (rather than experts) in this process.

Frankel and Levitt (2006), in a comprehensive review of the major postmodern approaches to psychotherapy, developed a set of guidelines for helping constructivist psychotherapists work with client resistance in ways consistent with constructivist thought. Below, I have summarized and adapted these guidelines for use in clinical supervision. Unlike a traditional psychoanalyst, who might attempt to facilitate supervisee transference by appearing as a blank slate, constructive supervisors place a strong emphasis on the value of empathic relationships for helping supervisees deal with resistance. The relationship-building strategies discussed earlier in this chapter, therefore, also form the foundation for addressing supervisee resistance. Additionally, constructive supervisors recognize that supervisee resistance to change is influenced and co-constructed by and through the relationship with the supervisor. Supervisors must, therefore, recognize how their own thoughts, feelings, insecurities, and cultural biases might be contributing to the ways in which supervisees approach and negotiate their resistances during supervision. An awareness of the interactional nature of resistance then allows supervisors to begin to help supervisees explore the potential goal of their resistance to change. In other words, constructive supervisors assist supervisees in identifying what their resistance is attempting to protect them from experiencing. Again, this is not done through skillful interpretation as in classic psychoanalysis, but through a caring, empathic stance of curiosity and inquiry. This same compassionate, inquiry-based approach can then be extended to help supervisees begin a process of reconciling their emerging desire to change and grow with their need for stability that rests in their existing ways of being.

Supervisee defense mechanisms can become especially apparent when viewing or discussing sessions they perceive as difficult or frustrating and can manifest in many different ways. I have, however, noticed a few patterns of defensive posturing among supervisees that can arise, which include counselors unconsciously failing to notice or attend properly to client statements (denial), recreating dynamics of their sessions with clients in supervision (parallel process), and reacting to clients based on their own unresolved issues (countertransference). Below I will briefly describe how to address these defense mechanisms in supervisees from a constructive approach.

Denial

One of the most striking examples of supervisee denial that often arises in beginning counseling students relates to issues of counselor discomfort regarding client emotions. Most beginning students recognize the importance of helping their clients get in touch with and express emotions; in fact, students often express this as a goal they have for their clients and something they would like assistance with during supervision. This is often followed with a declaration about their client's unwillingness or resistance to "go deep" with them or get in touch with their emotions.

When supervisees express this goal for their clients, it can be particularly useful to watch or listen to a tape of their counseling session together with the supervisee. Before the tape begins, the supervisor can frame the activity as an *experiment* in which both the supervisor and the supervisee can listen attentively for and make a list of the specific instances in which the supervisee has attempted to elicit an affect-oriented response from the client. The list will also include detailed descriptions of the ways in which the client has avoided these attempts to explore his or her emotion, which can include continually reframing the question to focus on thoughts or behaviors (instead of feelings), or switching the topic to an entirely new issue that is emotionally safer. This is an exercise that can often be useful in helping supervisees recognize how clients use defense mechanisms to avoid dealing with the issues that most likely brought them into therapy in the first place.

I have been amazed at how often the exercise actually highlights supervisee defense mechanisms at work, particularly *denial*. In many cases, our close inspection of the tape will reveal instances in which clients begin to respond genuinely and deeply to the counselor's affect-oriented approach. Surprisingly, rather than encouraging the clients to go deeper or even empathically acknowledging this disclosure, the counselor responds by redirecting the client back to discussing something emotionally safer, like asking for details about a particular event or their thoughts about the situation, rather than allowing the client to express their emotions more fully.

When this occurs, it can be useful to ask the supervisee to stop the tape and replay that section so both the supervisor and the supervisee can analyze the situation together. The process begins by asking the supervisee to carefully note the questions or behaviors that appeared to facilitate client disclosure of emotion. The supervisee is then asked to write down exactly what he or she did or asked to facilitate this emotional response. Next the supervisor can ask that they both listen attentively to the client reaction to this question or behavior and jot down the counselor's next response, which is often the response that directs the client away from emotion and back to some place safe. Generally, it is at this point that supervisees notice what had actually occurred: that the client was ready to move forward and express strong emotions and that they were the ones redirecting the issue to something safer. Some supervisees will initially try to defend their actions by making a clinical argument like, "I thought it was time to move on to something different that might be more meaningful to him." Others will contradict their earlier statement about the client not being willing to express emotion by stating that they actually thought the client was "not ready" for this type of emotional expression so they decided to redirect them to something safer. Amazingly, most supervisees state that they had not noticed this attempt by their clients to disclose emotional content before, even after having watched or listened to the tape numerous times prior to our supervision session. Seldom, in my experience, has a beginning supervisee, prior to our supervision session, noticed their role in keeping the session emotionally safe.

Early in my supervision career, I had attributed this type of supervisee behavior, which I had noticed regularly, as a simple mistake due to inexperience. In other words, I figured they just were not skilled enough to notice the opportunities they had missed. My response as a supervisor would be to point it out, tell them it was normal, and encourage them to do better next time. It was not until more recently, when I paid much closer attention to my supervisees' reactions to these "misses," that I was able to connect this recurrent issue to unconscious defense mechanisms at work.

We live in a society in which people are continually taught from infancy to hold in or "control" emotions; it is natural, therefore, that even those who may be highly suited to the profession will initially experience difficulties encouraging their clients to fully express their emotions in therapy. Supervisors cannot simply lecture or teach supervisees to be comfortable with strong emotions in clients. Rather, a much more detailed and experiential approach is needed to allow students to fully understand and experience that which is holding them back. This can include helping them take a comprehensive inventory regarding their experiences in dealing with the strong emotions of others, which often leads them to the conclusion that they were not as comfortable with these emotions as they originally thought. Supervisees can also be encouraged to discuss their own experiences in dealing with whatever the issue was that the client was discussing. Sometimes supervisees recognize, through this conversation, that they too are experiencing a similar dilemma or have dealt with something in the past and that they subconsciously avoided helping their client with it as a means of allowing themselves to also avoid addressing the issue.

Consistent with the constructivist approach to working with resistance, I do not provide interpretations as most psychoanalytic supervisors would. Rather, a constructive supervisor only needs to open a door for supervisee self-exploration of the issue by gently and empathically pointing out the inconsistency on the tape. The supervisor could say, for example, "You expressed a goal of wanting to get the client to express emotions in the session but we noticed that you changed the topic when the client started to do this." After that, the supervisor can simply allow space for the supervisee to explore the issue in whichever way he or she sees fit. While this approach takes more time than simply "teaching" what they missed, the awareness that some supervisees gain through this intervention has yielded strong, positive results in their future sessions—some even referring to the experience as providing a "breakthrough" for improving their future work.

Parallel Process

Another more commonly acknowledged form of supervisee resistance that is linked to Freudian notions of the unconscious is *parallel process*, which occurs when supervisees unconsciously present themselves in supervision in ways similar to ways in which their clients present to them during therapy (Bernard & Goodyear, 2014). One example is a supervisee who, while discussing or presenting a case of a client who is extremely agitated or scattered during therapy, may appear uncharacteristically agitated or scattered himself during supervision. It is believed that the parallel elements that the supervisee presents during supervision are somehow connected to unconscious elements of the client (i.e., they share the same problem) or can be indicative of the most concerning or frustrating aspects of the client's affect or presenting problem. In other words, supervisees may be so connected to or overwhelmed by the issues or behaviors of their clients that they unknowingly reenact this behavior with their supervisor. Moreover, supervision literature also recognizes that this process can be bidirectional in that dynamics in the supervisor/supervisee relationship can also manifest, through the supervisee, in the counselor/client relationship (Bernard & Goodyear, 2014). For example, problems in the relationship between supervisor and supervisee (e.g., supervisee resistance to the supervisor suggestions) can also manifest, through the parallel process, in the counselor/client relationship (client becomes resistant to suggestions from the counselor).

Consistent with constructivist notions of resistance, constructive supervisors recognize the potential for unconscious elements to enter into the supervisory relationship through parallel process and, as a result, pay attention to relational dynamics that may become mirrored in relationships between counselors/clients and supervisors/supervisees. Similar to the earlier example regarding resistance to dealing with strong client emotions, I have found it helpful to address this issue with supervisees by gently pointing out to them parallels that exist in these relationships. The above example of both the client and the supervisee demonstrating strong resistance to suggestions from the counselor and supervisor provides a useful example for illustrating this point. The supervisor could begin by first acknowledging the supervisee's frustration with his or her client by stating something like, "You seem frustrated by the fact that the client disregarded your suggestion to . . ." At this point, the supervisee would be provided an opportunity to expand upon his or her feelings of frustration, perhaps stating things like, "he doesn't seem to realize that this is for his own good" or "things would be better for her if she just followed this little piece of advice." After the supervisee has adequately expressed his or her thoughts and emotions regarding the interaction, the supervisor could then, as gently as possible, point out the fact that in a similar way, the supervisee has also, from time to time, disregarded suggestions from the supervisor. At this point, the supervisor may even offer a recent example of a suggestion he or she may have given that the supervisee disregarded. This can be followed with a brief description of the phenomenon of parallel process and an opportunity for the supervisee to discuss his or her reactions to this supervisor observation.

In my experience, this gentle process of noticing and pointing out instances of parallel process is all that is needed to allow supervisees to notice this phenomenon at work and reflect upon it. In most cases, supervisees, even those who are new to the profession, will engage in a thoughtful dialogue about the potential for parallel process to have impacted their experiences if it is presented in a way that is clear and that normalizes the phenomenon as a regular part of supervision for all counselors (even experts!). Sometimes these discussions happen immediately following my observation; other times the supervisee may appear to disregard the observation at that time only to bring it up in a later session after having thought more about it. Consistent with constructivist theory, the supervisor's job is merely to present the issue of parallel process for supervisees to consider; it is then up to the supervisee to decide whether or how much consideration the topic merits.

Countertransference

A third way in which supervisee defense mechanisms can manifest is a process Freud referred to as *countertransference*, which occurs when supervisees unknowingly react to clients based on their own unresolved issues. One example of countertransference that I have noticed frequently is when counselors are overly protective with clients, which can include counselors refusing to present appropriate challenges to a particular client during therapy or expressing needs to become overly involved as an advocate for the client. Some beginning counselors, as indicated in counselor developmental models, may demonstrate these behaviors with many clients as they struggle to transition from their roles as lay helpers. Helping beginning counselors learn to apply professional ethics and boundaries is not something that is always attributed to countertransference issues. However, issues of countertransference are often at play when the behavior, such as being overprotective with a client, appears inconsistent with their work with other clients. The counselor may, for example, have no problem confronting his older male clients and demonstrates this highly protective behavior only with one younger female client.

As with previous examples, constructivist supervisors begin to address potential countertransference issues with supervisees by gently pointing to the example. The supervisor could state, for example, "I noticed that you refrained from challenging this client on the inconsistency in her story." As Freud clearly demonstrated, it is normal for people to initially become angry or *defensive* when defense mechanisms are directly addressed. It would not be uncommon, therefore, for the supervisee to initially react negatively to this assertion. The counselor may, for example, state a clinical reason for not wanting to "push too hard" now because the client had been through enough already. While this may be true (clients often have lots going on while in therapy), it still begs the question from the supervisor as to why the counselor may be more hesitant to confront this client than he has been with some of his other clients. The supervisor could follow-up these questions by asking the supervisee if there are any people in his life who his client reminds him of. Supervisees, especially those newer to the profession, will sometimes express surprise at this question, at which point the supervisor can provide a brief explanation of countertransference. More experienced therapists, of course, know exactly where this question is headed.

It is worth repeating that constructive supervisors do not force supervisees to engage in a detailed discussion of countertransference issues. Their role is not to confront supervisees on these issues or to interpret them as some psychoanalytic therapists might. Rather, they seek to gently point out the issue and provide space for them should they be ready and willing to entertain the subject. Often supervisees will entertain the idea of countertransference and develop sophisticated ideas as to what might be causing them to react differently to one particular client. It is quite common, for example, for counselors who identify themselves as unconsciously attempting to protect a client to recognize similarities between their client and a loved one such as their own child, younger sibling, or spouse. They may also recognize, through this process, their own strong (and perhaps unfulfilled) need to care for and nurture someone like their client. These conversations, under the right conditions, can facilitate an incredible amount of growth and development in supervisees that will inevitably increase their self-awareness and ability to effectively help not only the client in mention, but also future clients. Other times, however, supervisees may not be ready to engage in this process for various reasons. In these cases, constructive supervisors can allow the session to continue without addressing the issue further while also reserving the right to introduce the topic in later sessions should the issue arise again.

Summary of addressing defense mechanisms in supervision

Addressing supervisee defense mechanisms such as denial, parallel process, and countertransference in supervision can be incredibly productive for supervisee professional growth. In fact, I have found that the failure to do so can result in supervisees remaining "stuck" in patterns that are not conducive to their own growth or the successful treatment of their clients. However, it is important to reiterate that constructive supervision involves much more than helping supervisees recognize and address unconscious blind spots or blocks. In fact, this aspect of supervision, from a constructive perspective, is secondary to the less directive, more autonomy-supportive and relationship-focused methods described earlier that focus on helping supervisees discover their own answers. Nonetheless, it can be especially tempting to devote more time than is necessary to this process when (1) supervisees express strong appreciation for uncovering unconscious material that manifests through therapy; and (2) supervisors gain feelings of satisfaction, mastery, and even superiority through it. In my own experience as a full-time faculty member, I have found it particularly tempting to mingle therapeutic elements into supervision to fulfill my own needs to sit in the counselor chair. Supervisors, as human beings, are also prone to defense mechanisms and blind spots and, as a result, need to be highly aware of how their own needs can interfere with what is best for their supervisees.

While not at the core of the constructive approach to supervision, elements of psychoanalysis, particularly denial, parallel process, and countertransference, can be useful in understanding supervisee resistance to change. Addressing supervisee defense mechanisms during supervision can, however, pose significant challenges to the supervisor as people often inherently resist attempts to recognize or confront defense mechanisms. Having a solid and trusting supervisor/supervisee relationship is crucial in allowing supervisees to feel supported enough to embark on this difficult task of self-discovery. Additionally, supervisees who have embraced mindfulness may be open to examining these deeper and more ingrained patterns of thoughts and behaviors.

Chapter Summary

In this chapter, four theories of counseling and psychotherapy were presented and elements of each that are relevant to constructive clinical supervision were described. At the core of the constructive approach are the core conditions outlined by Rogers for forming relationships with supervisees and providing a non-directive format that allows them to direct the sessions. These same principles are highlighted in SDT as ways of promoting intrinsic motivation and autonomy-supportive conditions. The principles of intrinsic motivation outlined in SDT are also useful in understanding when and how to deviate from a purely supervisee-centered approach, including when and how to give supervisees advice and compliments. Supervision can also be enhanced through mindful practices that allow supervisors and supervisees to be fully present and to non-judgmentally observe themselves. Finally, the constructive approach recognizes supervisee defense mechanisms that can inhibit change processes. Based on psychoanalytic principles, the constructive approach encourages supervisors to tentatively and gently highlight the presence of defense mechanisms and to patiently help supervisees explore their potential impact on their counseling and experiences in supervision.

References

Bernard, J.M. (1979). Supervisor training: A discrimination model. *Counselor Education and Supervision, 19,* 60–68.

Bernard, J.M., & Goodyear, R.K. (2014). *Fundamentals of clinical supervision.* Boston: Merrill.

Brown, A.P., Marquis, A., & Guiffrida, D.A. (2013). Mindfulness-based interventions in counseling. *Journal of Counseling and Development, 91,* 96–104.

Brown, K.W., & Ryan, R.M. (2003). The benefits of being present: Mindfulness and its role in psychological well-being. *Journal of Personality and Social Psychology, 84*(4), 822.

Chambers, R., Gullone, E., & Allen, N.B. (2009). Mindful emotion regulation: An integrative review. *Clinical Psychology Review, 29*(6), 560–572.

Chirkov, V., Ryan, R.M., Kim, Y., & Kaplan, U. (2003). Differentiating autonomy from individualism and independence: A self-determination theory perspective on internalization of cultural orientations and well-being. *Journal of Personality and Social Psychology, 84*(1), 97.

Christopher, J.C., & Maris, J.A. (2010). Integrating mindfulness as self-care into counselling and psychotherapy training. *Counselling and Psychotherapy Research, 10*(2), 114–125.

Deci, E.L. (1972). The effects of contingent and noncontingent rewards and controls on intrinsic motivation. *Organizational Behavior and Human Performance, 8*(2), 217–229.

Deci, E.L., & Ryan, R.M. (1991). A motivational approach to self: Integration in personality. In R. Dienstbier (Ed.), *Nebraska symposium on motivation. Vol. 38: Perspectives on motivation* (pp. 237–288). Lincoln, NE: University of Nebraska Press.

Frankel, Z.E., & Levitt, H.M. (2006). Postmodern strategies for working with resistance: Problem resolution or self-revolution? *Journal of Constructivist Psychology, 19*(3), 219–250.

Freud, S. (1949). *An outline of psychoanalysis* (J. Strachey, trans.). New York: W.W. Norton.

Grepmair, L., Mitterlehner, F., Loew, T., Bachler, E., Rother, W., & Nickel, M. (2007). Promoting mindfulness in psychotherapists in training influences the treatment results of their patients: A randomized, double-blind, controlled study. *Psychotherapy and Psychosomatics, 76*(6), 332–338.

Guiffrida, D.A., Lynch, M., Wall, A., & Abel, D. (2013). Do reasons for attending college affect academic outcomes? A test of a motivational model from a Self-Determination Theory perspective. *Journal of College Student Development, 54*(2), 121–139.

Hackney, H., & Goodyear, R.K. (1984). Carl Rogers' client-centered approach to supervision. In R.F. Levant, & J.M. Shlien (Eds.), *Client-centered therapy and the person-centered approach: New directions in theory, research, and practice* (pp. 278–296). New York: Praeger.

Hall, P.D. (1999). The effect of meditation on the academic performance of African American college students. *Journal of Black Studies, 29*(3), 408–415.

Hart, T. (2004). Opening the contemplative mind in the classroom. *Journal of Transformative Education, 2*(1), 28–46.

Hayes, S.C., Luoma, J.B., Bond, F.W., Masuda, A., & Lillis, J. (2006). Acceptance and commitment therapy: Model, processes and outcomes. *Behaviour Research and Therapy, 44*(1), 1–25.

Hayes, S. C., Strosahl, K.D., & Wilson, K.G. (1999). *Acceptance and commitment therapy: An experiential approach to behavior change.* New York: Guilford Press.

Kabat-Zinn, J. (1994). *Wherever you go there you are: Mindfulness meditation in everyday life.* New York: Hyperion.

Kirshenbaum, H. (2009). *The life and work of Carl Rogers.* Alexandria, VA: American Counseling Association.

Linehan, M.M., Cochran, B.N., & Kehrer, C.A. (2001). Dialectical behavior therapy for borderline personality disorder. In D.H. Barlow (Ed.), *Clinical handbook of psychological disorders: A step-by-step treatment manual* (pp. 470–522). New York: Guilford Press.

Mahoney, M.J. (2006). *Constructive psychotherapy: Theory and practice.* New York: Guilford Press.

Miller, J.J., Fletcher, K., & Kabat-Zinn, J. (1995). Three-year follow-up and clinical implications of a mindfulness meditation-based stress reduction intervention in the treatment of anxiety disorders. *General Hospital Psychiatry, 17*(3), 192–200.

Neimeyer, R.A. (1995). Constructivist psychotherapies: Features, foundations, and future directions. In R.A. Neimeyer & M.J. Mahoney (Eds.), *Constructivism in psychotherapy* (pp. 11–38). Washington, DC: American Psychological Association.

Patterson, C.H. (1997). Client-centered supervision. In. C.E. Watkins (Ed.), *Handbook of psychotherapy supervision* (pp. 134–146). New York: Wiley.

Reeve, J., Deci, E.L., & Ryan, R.M. (2004). Self-Determination Theory: A dialectical framework for understanding sociocultural influences on student. In D.M. Melnerney & S. Van Etten (Eds.), *Big theories revisited*, Greenwich, CT: Information Age Publishing.

Rogers, C.R. (1951). *Client-centered therapy: Its current practice, implications and theory.* Boston, MA: Houghton Mifflin.

Rogers, C.R. (1957). The necessary and sufficient conditions of therapeutic personality change. *Journal of Consulting Psychology, 21*, 95–103.

Rogers, C.R. (1980). *A way of being*. Boston, MA: Houghton Mifflin.

Rothaupt, J.W., & Morgan, M.M. (2007). Counselors' and counselor educators' practice of mindfulness: A qualitative inquiry. *Counseling and Values, 52*(1), 40–54.

Ryan, R.M., Lynch, M.F., Vansteenkiste, M., & Deci, E.L. (2011). Motivation and autonomy in counseling, psychotherapy, and behavior change: A look at theory and practice. *The Counseling Psychologist, 39*(2), 193–260.

Rybak, C.J. & Russell-Chapin, L.A. (1998). The teaching well: Experience, education, and counseling. *International Journal for the Advancement of Counseling, 20*, 131–139.

Schure, M.B., Christopher, J., & Christopher, S. (2008). Mind–body medicine and the art of self-care: Teaching mindfulness to counseling students through yoga, meditation, and qigong. *Journal of Counseling & Development, 86*(1), 47–56.

Segal, Z.V., Williams, J.M.G., & Teasdale, J.D. (2002). *Mindfulness-based cognitive therapy for depression: A new approach to preventing relapse*. New York: Guilford.

Siegel, R. (2011). West meets east. *Psychotherapy Networker*, Sept/Oct.

Skinner, B.F. (1953). *Science and behavior*. New York: Free Press.

Stone, D., Deci, E.L., & Ryan, R.M. (2009). Beyond talk: Creating autonomous motivation through self-determination theory. *Journal of General Management, 34*, 75–91.

Vansteenkiste, M., Zhou, M., Lens, W., & Soenens, B. (2005). Experiences of autonomy and control among Chinese learners: Vitalizing or immobilizing? *Journal of Educational Psychology, 97*(3), 468–483.

Watson, J.B. (1913). Psychology as the behaviorist views it. *Psychological Review, 20*, 158–177.

White, R.W. (1959). Motivation reconsidered: The concept of competence. *Psychological Review, 66*, 297–330.

Woodworth, R.S. (1921). *Psychology: A study of mental life*. New York: Holt.

3

THE PROCESS OF CONSTRUCTIVE SUPERVISION

In this chapter I provide a more detailed description of the process of constructive supervision, including describing the role that supervisors take (using Bernard's Discrimination Model) and the formats that are most conducive to facilitating supervisee autonomy and self-reflection from a constructive perspective. I then describe how supervisors can create space that encourages supervisees to deeply reflect upon their evolving theoretical orientations, and conclude by outlining how the constructive approach can be used to facilitate supervisee multicultural competence. Before beginning this more applied discussion, I offer a brief summary of the theoretical basis of the approach as described in Chapters 1 and 2 to conceptually ground the practice of constructive supervision.

Summary of the Theoretical Foundation of Constructive Supervision

As described in Chapter 1, constructive supervision is an integrative approach that is rooted in constructivist ideas of development, change, and learning. The constructive approach is based upon the following constructivist ideas about human growth and development:

- Knowledge is subjective and varies depending upon individual experiences.
- People have an inherent need to form relationships with others and much of the order we make of the world results from interpersonal relationships.
- Change is a necessary but difficult aspect of life and problems occur when we fail to make necessary changes.

- While we often desire balanced states, learning and growth occur best when we fall out of balance.

Constructive supervision is also based upon the following constructivist principles of learning:

- The most meaningful knowledge must be discovered rather than imparted from teacher to student.
- Learning is influenced not only by the current learning experiences, but also by predisposed notions derived from prior experiences.
- Language is central not only in communicating discoveries, but also in the process of discovery itself.
- Anxiety and mistakes can be central to the learning process when they are normalized and reflected upon.

As described in Chapter 2, constructive supervision also integrates principles from several theories of counseling and psychotherapy to facilitate these constructivist change processes. Central to the constructive approach is the need for supervisors to establish the core conditions outlined by Rogers, which include forming strong, empathic relationships with supervisees, and providing a non-directive format that allows supervisees to explore issues of meaning to them and develop their own answers. Constructive supervisors also seek to facilitate intrinsic motivation in supervisees by providing autonomy-supportive conditions as outlined in Self-Determination Theory. Additionally, constructive supervisors implement mindfulness-based practices that assist both supervisors and supervisees in being fully present and to non-judgmentally observe themselves and their clinical practice. Finally, the constructive approach integrates principles from psychodynamic theory as a means of assisting supervisees in observing how defensive mechanisms can inhibit change and growth.

Together, the principles of constructivist change, development, and learning outlined in Chapter 1 are integrated with elements of these four theories of psychotherapy to form the theoretical foundation for viewing supervision goals and implementing interventions from a constructive framework. In the next section, I will provide additional descriptions about the process of constructive supervision, beginning with identifying the role that supervisors take while implementing a constructive approach.

Supervisor Role

Supervision is a complex process that requires supervisors to perform a number of different roles to help facilitate supervisee development. According to Bernard's (1979) Discrimination Model, which is the most referenced and empirically supported model for conceptualizing the roles of the clinical supervisor (Bernard & Goodyear, 2014), supervisors can take one of three roles during supervision: teacher, counselor, or consultant. The *teacher* role is evident when supervisors provide direct instructions to supervisees, model appropriate counselor behavior, and provide evaluative comments of their work. According to Luke and Bernard (2006), the *teacher* role is used when supervisors believe a "less structured approach will leave the supervisee confused or somehow unable to access the supervision being provided" (p. 284). Supervisors acting in a *counselor* role focus on helping supervisees reflect on internal processes and reactions they may be experiencing during their sessions by reflecting and asking questions in ways that are consistent with psychotherapy. This role is useful when supervisors believe that internal issues may be interfering or clouding supervisee judgment or conceptualization. In the *consultant* role, the supervisor does not provide direct advice or direction, but encourages supervisees to develop and trust their own ideas and intervention strategies (Luke & Bernard, 2006). The *consultant* role, therefore, requires that supervisees take on much more responsibility for their own learning and development than when the supervisor is acting in the teacher or counselor roles.

Bernard (1979) asserted that successful supervisors incorporate and balance all three roles during supervision. The role that the supervisor takes at any given time, according to Bernard, depends upon the focus of the session (i.e., whether to develop intervention skills, conceptualization skills, or personalization skills) and the developmental needs of the supervisee. However, despite the fact that the Discrimination Model emphasizes the need to balance the three roles, Bernard and Goodyear, in their review of research examining the efficacy of the Discrimination Model, noted that *teacher* and *counselor* have emerged as the most clearly defined and prevalent of the three supervisor roles. Given the dominance of modernist and behaviorist approaches to learning in the field of counseling, which position the supervisor as expert, it is not surprising that the teacher role would receive so much attention from the field. It is also understandable, given that clinical supervision is conducted by counselors and psychotherapists, that the counselor role would also be highly visible during supervision. The consultant role, however, has remained "fuzzier" in the sense that it is less clearly defined and understood in clinical supervision literature, despite the fact that it is "intuitively appealing" (Bernard & Goodyear, 2014, p. 54).

While constructive supervisors can utilize all three supervisor roles, the *consultant* role is the most conducive for facilitating growth and change from the constructive model. Rather than seeking to impart knowledge to supervisees as a teacher, or focus on uncovering hidden internal processes as a counselor, constructive supervisors act primarily as *consultants* by providing conditions under which supervisees can identify issues of meaning to them and discover their own answers. The *consultant* role, in this sense, is consistent with constructivist ideas regarding the subjective nature of reality, the need for students to discover rather than receive knowledge, and the centrality of critical self-reflection to the learning process.

Below, I will describe how constructive supervisors facilitate supervisee autonomy and critical self-reflection using the consultant role. This is followed by a description of the ways in which constructive supervisors can integrate the teacher and counselor roles in ways that are consistent with these constructivist principles.

Consultant Role

Consistent with the person-centered approach to counseling (Rogers, 1957), supervisors acting in the consultant role must establish close, secure relationships with supervisees by providing unconditional positive regard, empathy, and congruence. As described in Chapter 2, unconditional positive regard can be established when constructive supervisors demonstrate trust in the abilities of supervisees to discover their own answers during supervision and provide them space for this learning to occur. At the core of this process is the use of reflective questions that assist supervisees in focusing more deeply on their understandings of clients and client issues, their internal reactions to and feelings about their clients, their hunches regarding potential intervention strategies, and their ability to evaluate the strengths and limitations of their approaches.

In the book *Supervision Strategies for the First Practicum,* Neufeldt (2007) provided numerous examples of questions that supervisors can ask to facilitate supervisee self-reflection in a number of areas. While Neufeldt's book is written for use with counseling students participating in their first practicum, most of the questions she suggests can be used to facilitate critical self-reflection in supervisees from any developmental level.[1] One example of how reflective questions can be used to facilitate supervisee development is to ask supervisees to critically reflect upon the questions that they asked their clients during therapy. Examples of reflective questions that can help supervisees think more deeply about their questions to clients include the following:

- What was going on for you when you asked that question?
- What were you hoping to learn from that question?
- How do you think the client reacted to that question?
- If you could say something different there, what might you say?

Supervisors can ask these questions directly to supervisees while watching their counseling sessions with them, or the supervisees can be asked to reflect upon these questions prior to their supervision session and to come to supervision prepared to discuss these reflections (see "Reflective Writing Activities" section in Chapter 4).

It is important to note that when asking reflective questions, supervisors need to ask questions for which they are genuinely seeking to gain an understanding of supervisees' perspectives and to allow supervisees space to critically reflect upon these perspectives. Problems can arise in supervision when the supervisor is trying to teach or give advice but does so by asking a question, which is a teaching style that teacher educators have referred to as "asking known information questions" (Mehan, 1979, p. 285). The following is a brief example of this problematic use of questioning in clinical supervision:

SUPERVISOR: What do you think the client was trying to communicate to you through this behavior?

SUPERVISEE: Hum, I don't know . . . maybe that she is not happy with her relationship at home?

SUPERVISOR: Well, maybe, but I think there is more going on here. Can you think of anything else she might be attempting to communicate through her behavior?

SUPERVISEE: I guess I'm not sure . . .

SUPERVISOR: Well, often clients will communicate to counselors in subtle ways. In this case, I think is trying to tell you something about how she is feeling about you, about the counselor/client relationship. Did you notice how she looked away when she said she was really pleased with the way her counseling sessions have been going?

SUPERVISEE: I can see that she looked away from me when she replied but I guess I didn't realize what that could have meant.

Clearly, the supervisor had something that he wanted to communicate to his supervisee. However, rather than simply stating it to the supervisee, he has attempted to elicit an answer from the supervisee using open-ended questioning. In cases like this, the supervisor is aware of the limitations of spoon-feeding answers to the supervisee; however, he is not yet trusting in the supervisee's abilities to develop her own answers, at least not the answers that he believes are right. Therefore, the supervisor ends up being caught in this intermediary role (which I sometimes refer to as "no-man's land") in which he asks known questions in an attempt to illicit the answer he wanted to tell the supervisee, but felt he should not. This process of asking *known information questions* can be incredibly frustrating for both supervisees and supervisors. Supervisees often leave these interactions feeling helpless and unable to "get it," which can greatly reduce their self-confidence and their abilities to reflect on the sessions during supervision. Likewise, supervisors also leave these interactions feeling frustrated as they struggle to get supervisees to answer the question correctly and think the way they want them to think without actually telling supervisees directly.

Rather than asking *known information questions*, constructive supervisors seek to draw answers from the supervisees themselves. This begins by seeking to understand supervisees' perspectives regarding elements of case conceptualization, interventions, or views of the client through the use of reflective questions. As constructive supervisors illicit supervisee perspectives, they assist supervisees in clarifying their perspectives and connecting these perspectives to other experiences. At the same time, constructive supervisors help supervisees explore not only the strengths of these perspectives, but also limitations so that they can develop new and more advanced ways of thinking. To illustrate this process, I will present the same scenario listed above from a more constructive perspective:

SUPERVISOR: Do you think the client was trying to communicate to you through this behavior?

SUPERVISEE: Maybe, I had not thought about it that way before, but she may be trying to tell me something here.

SUPERVISOR: What might she be trying to communicate do you?

SUPERVISEE: Perhaps, that she is not happy with her relationship at home?

SUPERVISOR: Okay, what aspect of this relationship might she not happy with?

SUPERVISEE: Well, she has mentioned before that she and her husband have not been getting along. This might be her way of sharing with me that she would like to talk more about it during our sessions?

SUPERVISOR: Okay, let's explore this a little further. Why might she have felt uncomfortable or been unable to share this directly with you?

Unlike the earlier example, the supervisor is not attempting to illicit a particular answer from the supervisee. Instead, the supervisor is drawing answers from the supervisee and asking the supervisee to think deeply about her answers. While they are covering the same issue as the earlier example, the second example is much more supervisee focused. Key to this process is a belief that (1) the supervisee is capable of coming to her own answers and (2) that there are multiple right answers. Once supervisors accept these two central assumptions, they are often better positioned to provide the type of space in which critical self-reflection occurs.

It is important to note that constructive supervisors, like constructive psychotherapists (Neimeyer, 1995), while seeking to understand the supervisees' perspectives, do not necessarily view these perspectives as static realities; rather, they view them as constantly evolving. Thus, constructive supervisors view all perspectives, both supervisees' and their own, as subject to constant change as the reflective process unfolds. Constructive supervisors encourage supervisees to explore new ideas freely, but also to view all new ideas as tentative hypotheses in need of future testing and reformulation rather than viewing them as absolute truths about their clients, themselves, or the psychotherapy process.

As described in Chapter 1, constructivists recognize that all change must be approached tentatively or people will resist because the new ideas can threaten the integrity of their existing worldviews (Neimeyer, 1995). Constructive supervisors can facilitate reflective thinking and risk-taking by using tentative language like *hypothesis* and *experiment* when framing the thinking of new ideas or in trying new things. Such tentative language can allow supervisees to consider new ways of thinking without feeling they need to completely abandon existing systems of meaning making. In this way, supervisors position themselves, not as authoritative experts, but as *co-experimenters* who seek to join supervisees in exploring their tentative hypotheses through the use of various experiments. This process can help supervisees think creatively by encouraging them to become more comfortable with uncertainty and risk-taking and less fearful of failure or harsh evaluations.

In addressing the role of uncertainty in constructivist counseling, Carlsen (1995) has stated that the goal for the counselor is to guide the client beyond "black-white, success-failure, and right-wrong models that suggest some sort of ultimate path" (p. 140). This allows the counselor to steer clients away from a fear of failure to a place where they are comfortable with uncertainty about outcomes. Carlsen (1995) continues by stating, "The challenge for psychotherapy is to encourage such creative enjoyments of the question of the growing, and of the avoidance of any fixed conclusions about what life (or in our case, psychotherapy) is all about" (p. 140). Similarly, this same goal of becoming less fixed on right or wrong and to develop a sense of curiosity, wonderment, and enjoyment in the process of observing and reflecting on one's own practice is also primary in framing outcomes in constructive supervision.

In addition to using reflective questions and tentative language to frame responses, constructive supervisors also serve in the consultant role by introducing reflective activities that are designed to promote supervisee reflection and creativity in areas that range from forming and maintaining relationships with their clients, conceptualizing cases and developing interventions, and understanding their own developmental progression as counselors. These activities, which I have described in detail in Chapter 4, can include metaphoric activities, mindfulness-based activities, and a number of constructivist psychotherapy activities that have been adapted for use in clinical supervision. Reflective-based activities can be especially fruitful during times when supervisees become frustrated or immobilized by apprehension or confusion. Rather than providing direct advice or compliments when supervisees struggle in developing their own answers, reflective-based activities can extend the opportunities for supervisees to creatively develop their own answers.

Teacher Role

While self-reflection through the use of the consultant role is at the core of the practice of constructive supervision, constructive supervisors can engage in some forms of more direct teaching by providing a limited amount of advice and instruction. Teaching must, however, be used sparingly and carefully so as not to risk instilling dependency on the supervisor or preventing supervisee reflective processes. The types of advice that are most helpful, from the constructive perspective, focus on instructing supervisees about how to be more reflective in their counseling process rather than providing them with direct advice on *how* to counsel. For example, a supervisor might provide the following directions on how to integrate reflective practice into the session: "If this comes up again, I want you to remember what you've come up with now and use that to help guide your intervention."

Constructivists recognize, however, that is impossible to be completely value or judgment free (Efram & Fauber, 1995). As counselors themselves, all supervisors, even the most dedicated constructivists among us, will undoubtedly encounter times when it can become difficult to resist the urge to provide direct instruction or advice to supervisees regarding how to proceed with clients. Sometimes an answer can be so clear to the supervisor that she or he may feel compelled to provide suggestions for supervisees who are unable to develop the answer on their own. At other times supervisors may feel, for various reasons, rushed to help the supervisee demonstrate a particular outcome with a client. The constructive approach allows supervisors to sparingly provide more active forms of advice about the counseling process if holding such insights to themselves begins to feel problematic.

It can be useful for constructive supervisors who are considering providing direct instruction to supervisees to carefully consider why a more directive approach is needed with their supervisees. As described in Chapter 2, it can be more effective to abstain from providing advice that derives from the need to demonstrate competence or superiority, or that seeks to privilege the supervisor's perspectives over those of the supervisee. Being mindful of one's motivations for providing advice can help supervisors sort out whether this direct instruction is what is best for the supervisee at this time. If the supervisor, after careful reflection upon his or her rationale, decides to provide direct instruction to the supervisee, there are ways of doing this that can minimize the deleterious effects of the direct instruction on supervisee autonomy, creativity, and critical self-reflection.

First, direct advice should only be offered after the supervisee has established strong abilities to think independently and to critically self-reflect. Providing direct advice early on can establish a pattern of dependency rather than one of autonomy and reflection. Second, it is important for supervisors to acknowledge that the perspectives they offer, like all perspectives, should not be taken as an absolute truth. Third, as described in the SDT section in Chapter 2, advice and direction need to be given with a clear and meaningful rationale, without force or coercion, and in a way that provides supervisees with choices about how and when to implement it. Fourth, framing the advice as a potential *experiment* for supervisees to try can be useful in allowing the advice to seem less threatening to the supervisee.

One example of how a supervisor could introduce a more active form of advice in a way that is consistent with constructivist principles of learning is the following: "The next time the client begins to talk about the loss of her child and you start to feel yourself becoming emotional, I'd like for you to try an experiment. Instead of fighting back your urge to cry, try allowing yourself to openly feel and express whatever emotions arise within you and just see what happens." Instead of directly telling the supervisee that it is okay to cry during the session, this approach encourages the supervisee to find out for herself how open expression of emotion can impact her session. Before conducting the experiment, supervisees should be provided space in the supervision session to openly and non-judgmentally discuss their reactions to the advice, including any reservations they have about it, and to formulate tentative *hypotheses* about what may occur should they chose to enact the advice. Supervisees who choose to proceed with the experiment can then be asked to come to the next supervision session ready to discuss the tentative results of their experiment with the supervisor.

The above scenario regarding providing advice to supervisees also provides an opportunity to highlight another important limitation of giving direct advice during supervision. The fields of counseling and psychotherapy are tremendously complex and, as a result, varied perspectives exist about numerous issues in the field, even among those within the same theoretical orientation. The issue presented in the preceding paragraph regarding the appropriateness of therapists crying with clients, for example, is something that can be conceptualized very differently depending upon which counselor you ask. Some may see crying with clients as the ultimate demonstration of empathy and, therefore, recommend that supervisees cry when they feel that level of emotion during sessions. Other counselors may feel that crying during sessions shows a lack of professionalism and could even demonstrate to clients that their issues are worse than they thought (if it makes my therapist cry, it must be really awful!).

The point of raising the issue is not to debate the merits of whether to cry or not during counseling sessions. Rather, I raise this issue to highlight that most aspects of counseling are too complex to be distilled into manuals and standard dos and don'ts. Inevitably, one piece of advice, no matter how appropriate at the time, will be contradicted at some point by someone else or found to be inappropriate under different circumstances. In my earlier days as a supervisor, I even noticed times when I would contradict my own advice during the same supervision session! The complexity of the counseling profession not only provides a strong rationale for supervisors to generally refrain from giving direct advice whenever possible, but also points to another important consultant role for the constructive supervisor: helping supervisees sort through the seemingly endless stream of conflicting advice and perspectives they encounter from various supervisors, instructors, colleagues, and counseling literature.

As described in the counselor development section of Chapter 1, dealing with seemingly conflicting advice can be overwhelming to some supervisees, especially counseling students and those who are early in their counseling careers. Rather than attempting to justify one piece of advice over another, constructive supervisors can play a pivotal role in helping supervisees sort through the confusion they experience when exposed to varying perspectives about the field. The use of reflective questions can be particularly fruitful in allowing supervisees to develop their own answers to complex issues for which they have received conflicting advice. Examples of such questions include the following:

- Why do you think your [colleague, professor, or supervisor] suggested that approach in this case but suggested something different later?
- Can you see anything different about this situation that might have caused the person to suggest this alternative route?

- Is there anything about this person's background or view of the profession that may have led him or her to suggest this particular approach?
- What client or contextual factors may have led you to receiving one piece of advice in this situation, and different advice in another situation?

By providing supervisees the opportunity to sort through what appears to be conflicting advice, they can not only gain a sense of how complex the field of counseling is, but also develop skills of critical self-reflection that will allow them to effectively navigate these complexities in the future.

A discussion of the teacher role also requires a brief review regarding when and how to provide compliments and praise when implementing a constructive approach to supervision. As described in the SDT section of Chapter 2, praise can be detrimental to promoting autonomy and self-reflection when supervisors use praise to motivate supervisees toward specific outcomes. Similar to the ways in which advice is given, constructive supervisors use praise and compliments sparingly and carefully during supervision. Rather than praising supervisee behaviors in their sessions (e.g., "Great job asking open-ended questions!"), constructive supervisors seek to offer praise for process-oriented achievements, which can include when supervisees demonstrate patience with themselves during supervision or self-reflective thinking. In this way, supervisors can positively reinforce self-reflective processes while maintaining supervisee competence and autonomy.

Additionally, constructive supervisors strive to provide conditions under which supervisees become comfortable assessing their own performance and development rather than providing them with external praise. In other words, rather than providing them with a compliment about their use of open-ended questions, a constructive supervisor might ask supervisees to provide their own assessments of their use of open-ended questions (e.g., "What did you think about your use of open-ended questions here?"). Prioritizing supervisee self-assessment in cases like this may seem counter-intuitive to many supervisors, especially those who were trained in more modernist formats that position the supervisor as the expert. After all, how could a supervisee possibly be able to see everything that a more experienced supervisor would see? Wouldn't some supervisees automatically assume they are doing fine and, therefore, rate poor performances highly? And wouldn't other supervisees be so critical of themselves that they need some compliments from supervisors to pick them up? These are excellent questions that I will address in much more detail in Chapter 5, which deals with the topic of assessment from a constructive perspective.

Counselor Role

Constructive supervisors also engage in selective use of the counselor role as a means of assisting supervisees in identifying how internal issues may interfere with their work with clients or their own development as counselors. Like the teacher role, the counselor role is one that constructive supervisors use sparingly and carefully with supervisees. Use of reflective questions such as "How are you feeling about this client?" or "Does discussing this issue bring anything up for you?" provide opportunities for supervisees to engage in the process of self-exploration regarding the potential influence of personal issues on their work with clients.

Effective use of the counselor role can be facilitated when supervisors normalize this process for supervisees by explaining to them early on the need for them to pro-actively self-explore personalization issues during supervision. Additionally, supervisors seeking to encourage supervisees to explore how their own issues may impact their work with clients may also provide supervisees with feedback that compliments their process of self-exploration. For example, the supervisor could compliment the supervisee on engaging in the process of self-exploration (e.g., "I appreciate how difficult it is to look at yourself in this way") or on the amount of self-knowledge they develop from their explorations (e.g., You seem to have really learned a lot about yourself through this process").

While many supervisees will readily engage in this process of self-exploration through the use of reflective questions, others will find it more difficult to relate their own personal issues to their work with clients. As described earlier in this book, this can be particularly difficult when they perceive themselves as experiencing change too rapidly or drastically. In these cases, defense mechanisms such as denial, parallel process, and countertransference can cause supervisees to resist engaging in the client role during supervision. When supervisees become hesitant or even resistant to exploring how their personal issues may be manifesting in their work with clients, supervisors can implement the suggestions provided in the psychodynamic section of Chapter 2. The section also includes suggestions for balancing the counselor role in a way that does not turn supervision into therapy for the supervisee.

In this section I have described how constructive supervisors utilize the consultant role to provide the conditions under which supervisees learn to critically self-reflect upon their work. While the teacher and counselor roles are also available when using constructive supervision, constructive supervisors maintain these other roles sparingly and implement them cautiously. In the next section, I discuss the various formats used in clinical supervision, which include the use of technology (e.g., live supervision, video recordings) and outline the formats that are most conducive for facilitating critical self-reflection from a constructive perspective.

Supervision Format

There are several formats that supervisors can use to structure clinical supervision, which include various forms of live supervision, audio or video tape review, and supervisee self-report of their counseling sessions (Bernard & Goodyear, 2014). While the constructive approach can be implemented using any of the aforementioned formats, some formats lend themselves better to facilitating supervisee development, growth, and change from a constructive perspective than others. As

I will describe below, formats that focus on monitoring supervisee performance and providing direct instruction to supervisees tend to be the least effective for implementing a constructive approach, while formats designed to facilitate critical self-reflection, creativity, and self-understanding are most conducive to assisting supervisee development from a constructive perspective.

Formats Focusing on Teaching and Monitoring

One supervision format that can be used to instruct and monitor supervisees is the "bug-in-the-ear" approach. In this format, supervisors utilize wireless microphones and earphones that allow them to communicate directly with supervisees during their sessions. Live supervision utilizing the bug-in-the-ear technology allows supervisors to provide regular instructions to supervisees during their sessions; compliments when they do things correctly; corrections when doing things the supervisor perceives as incorrect; and to monitor all aspects of the session, which can involve intervening in sessions when supervisors feel it is necessary to protect clients or facilitate counseling processes.

A second format that focuses on instruction and monitoring supervisee behavior is when supervisees submit audio or video recordings of their counseling sessions to the supervisor to review outside of the normal supervision session. When supervisors and supervisees meet for supervision, the sessions typically involve the supervisor providing written or oral feedback to supervisees regarding their performance on that particular tape, which includes outlining things the supervisees did well, things they need to improve upon, and tips for assisting them in conceptualizing and intervening.

These two formats of conducting supervision are largely consistent with behaviorist pedagogical principles since the main purposes are to monitor supervisee behavior and client welfare, and to teach (through reinforcement) the counseling processes that are consistent with the supervisor's preferred approach. While behaviorist approaches to supervision are useful for conveying information from supervisor to supervisee, the approaches can also prevent supervisees from developing critical thinking skills and new ways of conceptualizing their work with clients (Fong, 1998; Nelson & Neufeldt, 1998) and may even encourage supervisees to become dependent upon their supervisors for answers (Guiffrida, 2005). These behaviorist methods of monitoring and instructing supervisees are inconsistent, therefore, with the goals of constructive supervision, which prioritize supervisee autonomy, critical self-reflection, and creativity as central in facilitating supervisee growth, change, and development.

Formats Focusing on Autonomy, Reflection, and Creativity

Rather than seeking to monitor and instruct supervisees, constructive supervisors utilize technology in a way that facilitates supervisee autonomy, self-reflection, and creativity. Central to this process is the use of audio or videotapes in supervision, which have been used extensively throughout the history of the profession for counselor training and research; most notably, with the work of Carl Rogers (Kirshenbaum, 2009). However, rather than supervisees submitting tapes to supervisors for critique and evaluation, constructive supervisors watch these sessions *with* supervisees to facilitate a process of critical self-reflection. While the use of videotapes is preferable over audiotapes since they also allow supervisees to reflect upon counselor and client non-verbal behavior, audiotapes are also useful and can be more practical and less obtrusive to clients.

The most established and widely known method of clinical supervision that relies upon the supervisor and supervisee mutually viewing or listening to the supervisee's counseling sessions to facilitate supervisee reflection is Interpersonal Process Recall (IPR; Kagan & Kagan, 1990; Kagan & Kagan, 1997). IPR is based upon a developmental model that asserts that while people need one another, they are also hesitant to become too close to people for fear of being controlled, becoming dependent, or being judged negatively by others. According to Kagan and Kagan (1997), this inherent need to both connect with and fear others results in an "approach-avoidance syndrome" (p. 298), whereby people continually approach and retreat from intimacy with others. As a result of this need to both connect with and avoid meaningful contact with others, people often become "diplomatic" (p. 299) in conversations, paying attention and reacting only to safe and less intimate aspects of the conversation for fear of the other's emotions or of becoming too close to them, even though the more serious or intimate aspects are readily apparent to them through both verbal and non-verbal communication. People caught in this approach-avoidance communication pattern can also become attacking in their conversation styles as a means of protecting themselves from intimacy.

IPR is based on the premise that it is only through a process of establishing safe, intimate relationships that people learn to trust others enough to disclose vulnerabilities and to pay attention to the intimate aspects of their conversations. In IPR supervision, which they refer to as the *recall* session, the supervisor strives to provide the conditions under which supervisees re-experience their counseling session in a safe and supportive environment so that they can focus on the deeper meanings that clients were attempting to convey to them. These supervision sessions, therefore, focus exclusively on the supervisee thoughts and emotions about the session and the client.

In IPR, videotapes of the supervisees' counseling sessions are viewed together with the supervisor. However, rather than the supervisor directing the session by using segments of the tape to instruct the supervisee or providing evaluative comments, the supervisor acts as an *inquirer* to assist the supervisee in better understanding the dynamics of the session that may have gone unnoticed during the session. Supervisees are instructed to stop the tape frequently at any point they believe something important to be happening on the tape and to describe their thoughts and emotions at the time. The supervisor's role is to listen attentively and empathically to supervisees as they recall their thoughts, emotions, and hunches about the client; the interpersonal dynamics during the session; or any other information that becomes apparent upon watching the tape. The supervisor acts as an *inquirer* by asking questions designed to facilitate deeper reflection and understanding on the part of the supervisee. Such questions can include the following:

- How were you feeling about the client during this segment?
- How do you think the client perceived you here?
- What do you think he was trying to communicate to you?
- How did you want the client to perceive you?
- Do you recall any other thoughts going through your mind as this occurred?
- If you could go back and do it again, what might you do differently and why?

Several studies have proven the efficacy of IPR in facilitating clinical skill development and affective sensitivity in supervisees when compared to traditional didactic methods (Kagan & Krathwohl, 1967; Kagan & Kagan, 1997; Kingdon, 1975). IPR is especially useful in deepening counselor self-awareness regarding the counselor/client relationship (Cashwell, 1994). Additionally, IPR has been proven effective with counselors from various levels of skill and experience, from beginning trainees and paraprofessionals to seasoned experts (Bernard, 1989).

Given the strong emphasis of IPR in helping supervisees develop their own answers and in allowing hidden elements of the counseling sessions to emerge, IPR techniques are highly consistent with the constructive approach to supervision. In fact, IPR, in many ways, can be considered a core technique used by constructive supervisors. Yet despite the ability of IPR to foster reflective processes in ways consistent with constructivist ideas of growth and change, there are a number of salient limitations of the approach from a constructive perspective. First, IPR does not allow supervisors to provide direction, advice, or instruction to supervisees at any point, whereas the constructive approach provides options that allow supervisors to deviate from the consultant role without sacrificing supervisee autonomy and self-reflection. Second, IPR does not recognize the need for supervisors to actively address supervisee resistances to change using the counselor role. Third, IPR sessions must be conducted while watching videotapes, which is not always possible depending upon the setting in which the supervisee is working. While videotapes are preferable, constructive supervision can also occur with audiotapes or without tapes at all if conditions do not allow for taping. Fourth, IPR does not advocate for the use of reflective activities to facilitate supervisee reflection during periods in which supervisees become frustrated or immobilized.

Perhaps the most important limitation of IPR is that the focus of the sessions is almost entirely on interpersonal dynamics between supervisees and clients. While exploration of these dynamics can be incredibly valuable in helping supervisees develop strong relationships with clients and case conceptualization skills, these dynamics can be magnified to the point that they become overblown and distorted. In noting this limitation of IPR, Bernard and Goodyear (2014) stated: "what is a perfectly functional relationship can come to look somehow dysfunctional when overexposed, and as all persons in the helping professions know, some relationship dynamics are best left underexposed" (p. 164). These limitations inherent in IPR have led Cashwell (1994) to recommend that IPR be used in conjunction with other supervision approaches rather than recommending it as a sole approach.

While IPR techniques are central in allowing constructive supervisors to effectively operate within the *consultant* role, especially when exploring relationship dynamics that occur between supervisees and clients, the constructive approach seeks to extend IPR in ways that allow supervisors more flexibility and creativity in addressing the needs of supervisees. This can include exploring issues beyond counselor/client relational dynamics, gently pointing out and challenging supervisee defense mechanisms, and facilitating structured activities that can develop supervisee creativity and self-reflection during times when they find it difficult to develop their own answers. Another key difference between IPR and the constructive approach revolves around the role of counseling theory in supervision. In the next section, I will describe how constructive supervisors assist supervisees in developing and using counseling theory.

Role of Counseling Theory

In an earlier article (Guiffrida, 2005), I outlined a model for teaching counseling theories that I termed the *Emergence Model*. I developed this model based on the limitations I discovered in teaching counseling theories from a behaviorist perspective. Like a lot of other instructors, I began my counseling theories course by introducing students to each theory's historical origins, fundamental concepts and terminology, view of human growth and change, and intervention strategies through reading and lecture. After students became familiar with the language of the theories, I provided them with the opportunity to observe each theory in use through watching videos and by providing my own class demonstrations. Afterward, I incorporated experiential activities, which included case analyses, practice sessions with peers, and small group discussions in which students compared and contrasted the different approaches. I would then assess student learning through a combination of multiple choice exams and written essays in which students would critique the various theories or analyze cases using the theories. At the end of the course, students were required to write a paper in which they chose the theory or theories (if integrative) that seemed to fit best with them. This theory or theories would then serve as the lens through which they would view their early clinical experiences.

Prior to teaching this class, I served as a clinical supervisor for several years for master's degree-level students who were enrolled in their first counseling practicum. During our initial session, I would ask these supervisees to identify the theory or theories they had identified most with during their theories course (they had been trained in theories in a way similar to what I described above) and we would use this theory or theories as the guiding framework for viewing client issues and developing intervention strategies. I quickly noticed, however, that few of the students actually adhered to their espoused approaches; in fact, many of them did not do anything that remotely resembled the approaches they espoused at the beginning of the supervision experience. At the time, I attributed this to them not receiving adequate instruction in their theory course.

A few years later, while again serving as the supervisor of master's degree-level practicum students, I encountered some experiences that caused me to rethink this issue of how students develop their theoretical orientations and how supervisors can assist in this process. I once again noticed a high level of incongruence between these students' espoused theories and what they were doing with clients; however, this time the students were those who had taken my theories class! Even those who did extremely well in the class and wrote excellent papers outlining their preferred theoretical orientations failed to translate this learning into their real-world practice. Most astounding to me was one supervisee who expertly implemented a solution-focused approach with her client (one of her espoused theories), even going as far as asking the client the "miracle question." Rather than complimenting her on her execution of solution-focused therapy, I chose to first ask her what the approach was she was using. I was astonished to hear her say that she thought that segment of the tape demonstrated her use of Adlerian Therapy!

At this point, I knew it was time to rethink everything I was doing with regard to the way I taught counseling theory and how I addressed supervisee theoretical orientation during clinical supervision. It was clear to me that what resonated with students conceptually in books, lectures, and videos, was not necessarily what they ended up relying on in their actual practice with real clients. Rather, students seemed to disregard what they learned in class and rely, instead, on their own hunches and ideas that had developed from prior experiences. Rather than abandoning the use of theory in supervision, I sought to discover other ways of teaching it that embraced student prior knowledge and prioritized real-world experiences. This search led me to consider constructivist theories of learning and to develop the *Emergence Model* as a means of facilitating the development of counseling theory from a constructivist perspective. In addition to revolutionizing the way I taught counseling theories, these constructivist principles of learning also changed the way I approached and integrated counseling theories into my work as a supervisor.

In describing the role of theory in constructivist psychotherapy, Neimeyer (1995) asserted that any theoretical orientation can be a resource for the constructivist practitioner "as long as it is interpreted as a historically and culturally bounded set of provisional metaphors and guidelines rather than as an applied science that compels only a certain conceptualization of the problem and only a single, approved form of intervention" (p. 16). Similarly, constructive supervisors, based on an *Emergence Model* approach, value the role of counseling theory in assisting supervisees in conceptualizing client issues and developing intervention strategies. Like constructivist psychotherapists, however, constructive supervisors caution supervisees about viewing clients with the blinders of externally imposed perspectives or attempting to emulate the way others conduct psychotherapy.

Rather than assuming supervisees begin their counseling experiences with a firmly rooted espoused theory, constructive supervisors ask supervisees to become co-experimenters with them in observing and understanding their predisposed notions of human change and growth. This is not to say that supervisees should begin without an espoused theoretical orientation; but, constructive supervisors caution supervisees not to use these theories in ways that limit full exploration of their clients and themselves.

A major goal of constructive supervision is to assist supervisees in understanding how their preconceived notions, including notions about how problems occur and what their role as helpers should be, can impact on the ways in which they view their clients and decide upon interventions. Rather than asking supervisees to abandon these predisposed notions of helping, constructive supervisors strive to provide conditions under which these notions emerge so that supervisees can observe them, consider their origins, and delineate their strengths and limitations. Eventually, the constructive supervisor encourages supervisees to look to established theories that help explain their predisposed notions and to push them to consider new ways of thinking about their clients' issues and their roles as helpers.

The use of the consultant role and reflective questions, in particular, is central in facilitating supervisee reflective thinking regarding theories of counseling. This can begin early in the supervision experience by asking supervisees to articulate their understandings of human growth and development without connecting these views to established theoretical orientations. This conversation can occur even with more experienced supervisees, including those who are deeply entrenched in particular theoretical orientations prior to the supervision experience. In fact, asking experienced counselors to articulate their notions of human growth and change, and to disentangle these perspectives from the language of established theoretical orientations, can be especially useful to seasoned professionals who may have become disillusioned with their initial theory of choice or with theories in general. You will recall from Chapter 1 that these concerns are typical of counselors in the early professional and seasoned expert stages. Examples of reflective questions that can help supervisees explore their predisposed notions of human growth and change early in the supervision experience include the following:

- What do you believe to be necessary for people to develop and grow in healthy ways?
- What types of things tend to get in the way of healthy development?
- How did you come to these understandings?

- Why do you believe people come in for counseling?
- What do you believe your role as a helper to be?

Another way to help supervisees creatively reflect upon their predisposed notions of human growth and change is to ask them to describe, either in writing or verbally with the supervisor, a difficult change that they recently made in their lives. In their descriptions, supervisees should also describe challenges they encountered while attempting to make the change, as well as things that helped support or facilitate the change. This brief reflective activity can assist supervisees in recognizing the knowledge they already possess regarding human change processes and how this knowledge impacts the ways in which they assess and intervene with clients.

Key to this process is that supervisors establish a safe and secure relationship with supervisees and that they explain their rationale for encouraging supervisees to explore their predisposed notions of human growth and change. Beginning students may feel overwhelmed by being asked such sophisticated questions so early in their training. This anxiety can be heightened by the fact they will be held accountable, in a sense, to these views since they will analyze the extent to which these views are manifested in their clinical work. Conversely, more experienced counselors may feel these types of questions are too basic to be of use to them, especially if they already possess a deep understanding of and adherence to a particular theoretical approach. Supervisors can allay these concerns by carefully explaining the constructivist perspective about change and growth, including the notion that they themselves are also changing as a result of their counseling and supervisions experiences, and by encouraging them to use tentative language when articulating these new understandings.

Once supervisees articulate and clarify with the supervisor their predisposed notions of human growth and change, they can then begin to examine the extent to which these views influence their work with clients using the same reflective process. Examples of reflective questions that can assist supervisees, of any developmental level, in critically reflecting upon the ways in which their predisposed notions of human growth and change influence their views of their clients, and of psychotherapy more broadly, include the following:

- What do you believe to be going on with the client right now and what factors do you see as contributing to this problem?
- How do these issues relate to larger issues of change and growth that you have experienced yourself or noticed in other clients?
- How do you know this to be true? What evidence do you have to support this hypothesis?
- Why might this hypothesis not be true? What, if any, evidence could suggest an alternative explanation?

- If there is a possible alternative explanation, what might that look like and how might you test this alternative explanation?

Once supervisees begin formulating tentative hypotheses about their clients, the supervisor can suggest that supervisees begin referring to established theories to help them clarify and further understand the theories they have begun to articulate. With well over 400 hundred theories of counseling to choose from (Karasu, 1986), there is certainly no shortage of options for supervisees to consider. Undoubtedly, there is an established theory that closely resembles the tentative hypotheses the supervisee has developed. This can be their espoused theory, or something totally new. Regardless of which theory the supervisee chooses, it is important to note that the supervisor does not need to be an expert on the theory. While supervisors may provide some suggestions on where supervisees can begin their searches (which can be especially helpful to newer counselors with less knowledge of counseling theories), the supervisor serves only as a facilitator in this process, not as an expert or guide. Serving purely as a facilitator, the supervisee can frame this assignment as a question that the supervisee needs to uncover using all the clues that have emerged during the supervision session.

As supervisees begin to discover and articulate theoretical orientations that help explain and expand their predisposed notions of human growth and change, the supervisor continues to use reflective questions to help them clarify how they know this to be true and to push them to consider what the implementation of such an approach would look like in practice with their current clients. This includes asking them about potential strengths of the approach and limitations. Once a picture of this process begins to emerge for supervisees, the supervisee may then feel prepared to implement and reflect upon this new intervention.

This process can look very different depending upon the needs of the supervisees. For some, it can be a transformative experience as they tentatively explore totally new ways of understanding their clients and the world. For others, it may simply reinforce their prior ways of being with clients, including solidifying their adherence to the theory they originally espoused. Either outcome is considered successful as long as supervisees authentically engaged in this reflective process and emerge from it with a more thoughtful and well-developed understanding of how their evolving notions of human growth and change affect the ways they conceptualize client issues and develop intervention strategies.

Facilitating Supervisee Multicultural Competence

In addition to helping supervisees better understand and develop their theoretical orientations, another central aspect of constructive supervision is to facilitate multicultural competence in supervisees. Fortunately, the constructivist theories of human growth and change upon which the constructive approach to supervision is based are closely aligned with current conceptualizations of effective multicultural counseling and supervision. These concepts include valuing multiple perspectives of reality; recognizing the interconnectedness of human meaning-making processes; providing empathic, autonomy-supportive relationships with supervisees; and helping supervisees embrace fear and anxiety as necessary perquisites to meaningful change. Below I will elaborate on how each of these fundamental elements of constructive supervision can be applied to facilitate multicultural competence with supervisees.

The most salient aspect of constructive supervision, from a multicultural perspective, is the epistemological view regarding the relative nature of knowledge and truth. Truth, from a constructivist perspective, merely reflects the values and norms of a particular person or group at one particular time and place. As D'Andrea (2000) has stated, "By insisting that 'knowledge' and 'truth' are relative constructs that are significantly impacted by the historical period and cultural context of which one is a part, postmodernism and constructivism help individuals liberate themselves from the sort of egocentric and ethnocentric tendencies that have characterized most of human society "(p. 3). Constructivism, therefore, provides a powerful, multicultural lens from which to conduct supervision by legitimizing beliefs from diverse groups. In fact, Hansen (2010) has asserted that the entire multicultural counseling movement is dependent upon constructivist theory because "without the epistemological possibility of multiple, legitimate realities, diversity, as a value, would be nonsensical" (p. 101).

At the same time that constructivists recognize the fallibility of *reality* and *truth*, they also recognize the harm that many of the ideas held by members of dominant groups can have on members of non-dominant groups. It is for precisely this reason that constructivist counselors seek to uncover the hidden ways in which current understandings of reality and truth can shape power dynamics, and the harmful effects that current distributions of power can have on marginalized groups (Neimeyer, 2009). Constructivist ideas regarding the legitimacy of multiple realities provide constructive supervisors a framework for assisting their supervisees in questioning established understandings of power dynamics, and recognizing how these realities can shape views of what is considered healthy or normal.

Constructivists, while recognizing the potential for members of particular groups to share perspectives about reality based on common experiences within these groups, also reject essentialized notions of how cultural backgrounds influence worldviews. As Rigazio-Digilio, Goncalves, and Ivey (1996) cautioned, there is "as much variation within the same ethnic group as there is among different ethnic groups" (p. 243). Constructive supervisors recognize the need to understand clients and supervisees in context, which includes learning about how their understandings of the world have been shaped by their cultural backgrounds, as well as recognizing how their unique experiences distinguish their views from other members of their perceived in-groups. This constructivist perspective of reality, when applied to clinical supervision, encourages both supervisees and supervisors to become inquisitive about the influences of culture and experience on their clients' and their own views, while cautioning them against making assumptions based on essentialized notions of culture.

In addition to valuing multiple perspectives of reality and attempting to understand people in context, constructivist ideas can also help supervisors facilitate multicultural sensitivity in supervisees by recognizing the interconnectedness of human existence and meaning-making processes. Constructivists believe that the *self* does not develop in isolation, but in relationship to and with others. Like constructivist counselors, constructive supervisors work *with* (rather than *on*) supervisees to assist them in deconstructing their existing frames of reference and co-constructing new realities about themselves and their clients. These new understandings are not created solely by supervisees, nor are they imposed upon supervisees by their supervisors; rather, supervisee views about themselves and others are framed as constantly evolving as a result of their experiences in therapy *and* supervision. Supervisees' conceptualizations of themselves and their clients, therefore, are not viewed as static realities, but as evolving narratives that are co-constructed with the supervisor. This recognition regarding the vital role of the supervisor as a collaborator in the supervisees' multicultural development highlights the need for supervisors to actively recognize their own cultural biases and how these biases can impact the multicultural development of their supervisees.

Another aspect of the constructive approach to supervision that is conducive to facilitating multicultural competence during supervision is the emphasis on providing a warm, empathic, non-judgmental relationship that seeks to diminish power differentials between the supervisor and the supervisee. In fact, research suggests that the creation of this type of supervisory relationship may be the most important ingredient in facilitating multicultural competence in supervisees (Dressel, Consolli, Kim, & Atkinson, 2007). As described earlier in this chapter, constructive supervisors seek to minimize the potentially stifling effects inherent in hierarchical relationships by empowering supervisees to become the experts on their clients. By providing warmth, empathy, and autonomy, constructive supervisors seek to foster relationships with supervisees that encourage them to openly discuss their perceptions of difference and to actively explore their own biases in ways that are not only non-threatening, but also seek to instill in them a sense of excitement about creatively exploring the nature and impact of these biases without harsh judgment.

Similarly, the constructive focus on helping supervisees embrace ambiguity and anxiety, rather than seeking to minimize it, is another aspect of the constructive approach that is central in facilitating multicultural competence in supervisees. Research indicates that supervisees are often hesitant to address issues of diversity during clinical supervision (Bernard & Goodyear, 2014). From my experience, much of this hesitancy stems from their fears of being perceived by their supervisors as culturally ignorant, or, even worse, as racist, sexist, ageist, ableist, or any other label that signifies insensitivity on their part toward people of different groups. This fear of being labeled or viewed negatively can prevent supervisees from openly engaging in meaningful conversations that allow them to begin to recognize how their own biases may be impacting their perceptions of and work with their clients.

Rather than criticizing or labeling supervisees as they explore their own biases, constructive supervisors seek to normalize the fear and anxiety that often accompany these challenging experiences. Multicultural supervision, from a constructive perspective, is most effective when supervisors accept all supervisee thoughts and feelings regarding cultural differences, no matter how critical or painful, and help their supervisees to accept themselves. This is not meant to imply that supervisors should uncritically accept hateful or even stereotypical assumptions that supervisees may express; rather, the constructive supervisor accepts these ideas as legitimate for them given their prior circumstances and surroundings. This accepting stance can allow the constructive supervisor to help supervisees assume responsibility for their prior views and behaviors, which is a necessary step along their path toward becoming more multiculturally competent.

Similarly, constructive supervisors, having a firm grounding in constructivist views of change, also recognize that supervisees can resist changes that are perceived as too drastic for them at that moment. Resistance to change can be particularly relevant when supervisees begin the process of deconstructing ingrained biases that may have pervaded their thinking for much of their lives. Rather than viewing all instances of resistance as signs that they are unfit for the field, constructive supervisors accept supervisee resistances as a necessary step in the supervisee's evolution toward cultural competence. Supervisees may, for example, deny that biases have affected their work in any way one week, only to arrive at supervision ready to meaningfully deconstruct the experience in a subsequent meeting. As I have stated throughout this book, this stance is not one that lets supervisees off the hook for possessing biases. On the contrary, exploration of supervisee biases and the impact of these biases is a heavy focus of the constructive approach. However, in the constructivist tradition, constructive supervisors believe these conversations become more powerful when supervisees are given latitude to approach change safely and at their own pace.

The supervisor roles and functions that are inherent in the constructive approach can provide a strong foundation from which to facilitate cultural competence in supervisees. However, strong stigmas associated with sharing personal biases, combined with the fact that many people do not know how to effectively and sensitively talk about issues of diversity, can create barriers that prevent supervisees from raising the topic themselves. In fact, research suggests that if supervisors do not raise multicultural issues during supervision, the topic is often not discussed at all (Duan & Roehlke, 2001; Gatmon et al., 2001). In order to ensure that multicultural issues arise during supervision, it is important that constructive supervisors emphasize supervisee multicultural competence as a priority of the supervision experience. Additionally, it is widely accepted as best practice for supervisors to raise the issues of multiculturalism and diversity in their initial meetings with supervisees, in writing in their disclosure materials, and in continually raising the issue throughout the supervision experience (Bernard & Goodyear, 2014; Borders & Brown, 2005). Raising the topic of multiculturalism early in supervision not only signifies the importance of considering culture, difference, and biases as part of the supervision process, but can also improve supervisor/supervisee rapport by easing the discomfort that some supervisees may feel when this important aspect of supervision remains unaddressed (McRoy, Freeman, Logan, & Blackmon, 1986).

Consistent with these recommendations, constructive supervisors raise the issue of multiculturalism carefully with supervisees beginning in their first meeting. This includes clearly describing the expectation that supervisees increase their multicultural competence as a result of the supervision experience. Constructive supervisors may also choose to present supervisees with a list of multicultural learning objectives to help frame their experiences in supervision. The following are examples of multicultural objectives that can be shared with supervisees (drawn from D'Andrea, 2000):

- To critically deconstruct the ways in which traditional theoretical approaches and diagnostic criteria may fail to account for the ways that clients from different cultural backgrounds construct their experiences.
- To develop intervention strategies that reflect sensitivity to and respect for client cultural differences.
- To openly explore how their own biases can impact the ways in which they view their clients' issues.
- To consider the multicultural competences they will need to continue to develop to effectively counsel clients from diverse backgrounds.

Inherent in these multicultural learning objectives is the need for supervisees not only to broadly attend to issues of diversity, but also to attend to specific multicultural elements, which includes deconstructing their own theoretical approach from a multicultural perspective and to consistently notice how their own biases impact on their views of their clients. Most importantly, the objectives encourage supervisees to consider their limitations and to begin to identify additional training or experiences that can help them along their path.

In addition to describing these multicultural learning objectives with supervisees during the first meeting, constructive supervisors can also include multicultural learning objectives in their disclosure statements and evaluation materials. Supervisees can also be instructed at the initial supervision meeting to consciously attend to multicultural issues and concerns at some point throughout each of the subsequent supervision meetings. It can also be helpful for supervisors to share with supervisees that they recognize that raising these issues may initially be difficult for them and that the supervisor will assist them in this process by occasionally asking questions that address issues of diversity, difference, or personal biases. Supervisors may also choose to discuss with supervisees some of their own struggles in developing multicultural sensitivity and competence. This type of discussion, in addition to creating a more egalitarian relationship, also helps frame multicultural competence as a developmental process, rather than as an elusive endpoint. In fact, research suggests that supervisor self-disclosure about their own vulnerabilities, struggles, and learning can be comforting to supervisees who are nervous about discussing multicultural issues (Hird, Cavalieri, Dulko, Felice, & Ho, 2001).

Consistent with the other aspects of the constructive approach described earlier in this book, constructive supervisors attempt to refrain from providing direct advice or recommendations about how supervisees should view clients and themselves from a multicultural lens. Rather, they assume the role of a consultant who facilitates a dialogue designed to allow supervisees to develop their own answers about multicultural issues that arise during counseling and supervision. As I have stated throughout this book, this does not equate to letting supervisees ignore multicultural issues or to settle on culturally biased views of their clients. Rather, the constructive supervisor continually reminds supervisees to consider multicultural issues and biases and to critically evaluate and assess their stances throughout their development. This process allows supervisors and supervisees to co-construct unique understandings of their client problems that allow them to carefully attend to each client's unique individual and cultural backgrounds. Some examples of reflective questions that can be useful in facilitating cultural awareness in supervisees include the following:

- What elements of your own cultural background may influence your goals of therapy or your expectations of supervision?
- How might your cultural background impact the ways in which you view your client?
- How do you feel working with a person from a different race or cultural background?
- How might a client of a different race or cultural background feel about working with you?

Another useful way of introducing the topic of multiculturalism during clinical supervision is by exploring cultural differences between the supervisor and the supervisee. For example, Hird et al. (2001) offered the possibility of directly, yet carefully, pointing out cultural or demographic differences that exist between the supervisor and supervisee and asking supervisees their perceptions of how these differences could affect the supervision relationship. This process of carefully considering the impact of cultural differences on the supervisory relationship can then extend to helping supervisees consider how the same dynamics may be affecting their relationships with their clients.

One additional consideration that is important to note is for supervisors to carefully attend to the ways in which they introduce multicultural issues into the supervision process. While research strongly supports the need for supervisors to persistently address culture during supervision, research also suggests that supervisors can be ineffective in promoting multicultural competence in supervisees if they appear hypersensitive to cultural differences or overzealous about introducing diversity as a prevailing factor all the time (Leong & Wagner, 1994). While multicultural issues need to be addressed persistently, constructive supervisors will be most effective in facilitating multicultural competence when they establish a strong, empathic relationship with supervisees and demonstrate patience and acceptance when assisting supervisees in exploring potential biases, fears, and resistances.

In summary, the constructivist ideas of human growth, change, and learning that are inherent in the constructive approach to supervision lend themselves well to facilitating multicultural competence in supervisees, provided that supervisors raise multicultural issues frequently and sensitively. The constructivist view regarding the relative nature of reality encourages both supervisees and supervisors to seek to understand people in context, which includes exploring how both cultural norms and individual experiences can shape worldviews. By establishing an empathic, caring, and non-judgmental relationship in ways consistent with the constructive approach, constructive supervisors encourage supervisees to be inquisitive and excited in exploring the complex ways in which their cultural norms and biases, combined with those of their clients and supervisor, can affect their counseling practice.

Chapter Summary

In this chapter I have provided a more detailed description of the process of constructive supervision. Consistent with the theories reviewed in Chapters 1 and 2, constructive supervisors seek to facilitate supervisee autonomy, self-reflection, and creativity by functioning primarily as consultants who provide conditions under which supervisees can discover their own answers. I have also described how constructive supervisors engage in the teacher and the counselor roles in ways that facilitate, rather than hamper, the reflective process for supervisees. Also covered was how constructive supervisors can review audio or videotapes with supervisees in ways that facilitate these reflective processes. Additionally, I described how constructive supervisors help supervisees develop and critically reflect upon their theoretical orientations through understanding how their predisposed notions of human growth and change impact the ways in which they view their clients' issues and develop intervention strategies. Finally, I described how the constructive approach can be used to effectively facilitate supervisee multicultural development.

While the strategies presented in this chapter are often enough to allow most supervisees to discover their own answers during supervision, there are times when supervisees can become stuck and the answers become more difficult for them to discover on their own. In the next section, I will describe how supervisors can implement reflective-based activities that can assist supervisees in discovering their own answers when the strategies described in this chapter appear insufficient.

Note

1 Readers are encouraged to review Neufeldt's (2007) *Strategies for Supervising Students in the First Practicum* for additional examples of questions that can facilitate supervisee critical self-reflection.

References

Bernard, J.M. (1979). Supervisor training: A discrimination model. *Counselor Education and Supervision, 19*, 60–68.

Bernard, J.M. (1989). Training supervisors to examine relationship variables using IPR. *The Clinical Supervisor, 7*(1), 103–112.

Bernard, J.M., & Goodyear, R.K. (2014). *Fundamentals of clinical supervision*. Boston: Merrill.

Borders, L.D., & Brown, L.L. (2005). *The new handbook of counseling supervision*. New York: Routledge.

Carlsen, M.B. (1995). Meaning making and creative aging. In R.A. Neimeyer, & M.J. Mahoney (Eds.), *Constructivism in psychotherapy* (pp.127–154). Washington, DC: American Psychological Association.

Cashwell, C.S. (1994). Interpersonal process recall. *ERIC Digest, EDO-CG-94-10.*

D'Andrea, M. (2000). Postmodernism, constructivism, and multiculturalism: Three forces reshaping and expanding our thoughts about counseling. *Journal of Mental Health Counseling, 22*(1), 1–16.

Dressel, J.L., Consoli, A.J., Kim, B.S., & Atkinson, D.R. (2007). Successful and unsuccessful multicultural supervisory behaviors: A Delphi poll. *Journal of Multicultural Counseling and Development, 35*(1), 51–64.

Duan, C. & Roehlke, H. (2001). A descriptive "snapshot" of cross-racial supervision in university counseling center internships. *Journal of Multicultural Counseling and Development, 29*(2), 131–146.

Efran, J.S., & Fauber, R.L. (1995). Radical constructivism: Questions and answers. In R.A. Neimeyer, & M.J. Mahoney (Eds.), *Constructivism in psychotherapy* (pp. 275–304). Washington, DC: American Psychological Association.

Fong, M.L. (1998). Considerations of a counseling pedagogy. *Counselor Education and Supervision, 38*, 106–112.

Gatmon, D., Jackson, D., Koshkarian, L, Koshkarian, L, Martso-Perry, N., Molina, A., Patel, N. & Rodolfa, E. (2001). Exploring ethnic, gender, and sexual orientation variables in supervision: Do they really matter? *Journal of Multicultural Counseling and Development, 29*(2), 102–113.

Guiffrida, D.A. (2005). The emergence model: An alternative pedagogy for facilitating self-reflection and theoretical fit in counseling students. *Counselor Education and Supervision, 44*, 201–213.

Hansen, J. (2010). Consequences of the postmodernist vision: Diversity as the guiding value for the counseling profession. *Journal of Counseling and Development, 88*(1), 101–107.

Hird, J.S., Cavalieri, C.E., Dulko, J.P., Felice, A.A.D., & Ho, T.A. (2001). Visions and realities: Supervisee perspectives of multicultural supervision. *Journal of Multicultural Counseling and Development, 29*(2), 114–130.

Kagan, H., & Kagan, N.I. (1997). Interpersonal process recall: Influencing human interaction. In C.E. Watkins (Ed.), *Handbook of psychotherapy supervision* (pp. 296–309). New York: Wiley.

Kagan, N.I., & Kagan, H. (1990). IPR—A validated model for the 1990s and beyond. *The Counseling Psychologist, 18*(3), 436–440.

Kagan, N.I., & Krathwohl, D.R. (1967). *Studies in human interaction: Interpersonal process recall stimulated by videotape.* East Lansing, MI: Michigan State University.

Karasu, T.B. (1986). The specificity versus nonspecificity dilemma: Toward identifying therapeutic change agents. *American Journal of Psychiatry, 143,* 687–695.

Kingdon, M.A. (1975). A cost/benefit analysis of the interpersonal process recall technique. *Journal of Counseling Psychology, 22*(4), 353.

Kirshenbaum, H. (2009). *The life and work of Carl Rogers.* Alexandria, VA: American Counseling Association.

Leong, F.T., & Wagner, N.S. (1994). Cross-cultural counseling supervision: what do we know? What do we need to know? *Counselor Education and Supervision, 34*(2), 117–131.

Luke, M., & Bernard, J.M. (2006). The school counseling supervision model: An extension of the discrimination model. *Counselor Education and Supervision, 45*(4), 282–295.

McRoy, R.G., Freeman, E.M., Logan, S.L., & Blackmon, B. (1986). Cross-cultural field supervision: Implications for social work education. *Journal of Social Work Education, 22*(1), 50–56.

Mehan, H. (1979). "What time is it, Denise?": Asking known information questions in classroom discourse. *Theory into Practice, 18*(4), 285–294.

Neimeyer, R.A. (1995). Constructivist psychotherapies: Features, foundations, and future directions. In R.A. Neimeyer & M.J. Mahoney (Eds.) *Constructivism in psychotherapy* (pp. 11–38). Washington, DC: American Psychological Association.

Neimeyer, R.A. (2009). *Constructivist psychotherapy: Distinctive features.* New York: Routledge.

Nelson, M.L., & Neufeldt, S.A. (1998). The pedagogy of counseling: A critical examination. *Counselor Education and Supervision, 38,* 70–88.

Neufeldt, S.A. (2007). *Supervision strategies for the first practicum* (3rd ed.). Washington, DC: American Counseling Association.

Rigazio-DiGilio, S.A., Gonçalves, O.F., & Ivey, A.E. (1996). From cultural to existential diversity: The impossibility of psychotherapy integration within a traditional framework. *Applied and Preventive Psychology, 5*(4), 235–247.

Rogers, C.R. (1957). The necessary and sufficient conditions of therapeutic personality change. *Journal of Consulting Psychology, 21,* 95–103.

4

REFLECTIVE ACTIVITIES

As outlined in Chapter 3, the consultant role is central in constructive supervision. Supervisors who maintain a consultant role by establishing strong relationships with supervisees and posing reflective questions to them are often able to provide the conditions necessary for supervisees to discover their own answers during supervision. These self-discovered answers can be more meaningful and powerful than answers that are handed down to them from supervisors. As a result, constructive supervisors attempt to refrain, as much as possible, from engaging in traditional teaching practices, like providing direct advice about how to counsel.

There are instances, however, when even the most self-reflective supervisees can experience difficulty in developing their own answers during supervision. This can occur when supervisees become immobilized by apprehension, overwhelmed by a seemingly endless array of options, or simply frustrated by the reflective process. Some counselor development literature suggests that in these cases, supervisors should deviate from the consultant role and take a more active, teaching approach (Bernard & Goodyear, 2014). A constructive approach, however, asserts that supervisees should be continually encouraged to develop their own answers, even in cases when these answers do not come easily to them. Rather than abandoning the reflective process, supervisors operating from a constructive approach can utilize reflective-based activities that encourage supervisees to creatively approach their problems in new ways.

In this chapter, I offer a number of activities that supervisors can use to facilitate supervisee self-reflection during times when supervisees experience difficulty in developing their own answers. Each activity provides potential for supervisees to discover their own answers using a different medium, which range from various forms of artistic and written expression, to mindful attention to one's breath. These activities include metaphoric drawing activities, reflective writing exercises, metaphoric representation using the sand tray, verbal reflections while closely examining their clients faces, and mindfulness-based activities. I will also provide guidelines for introducing the activities, adapting the activities for use in both individual and small group supervision, and for conducting the activities in ways that are consistent with constructivist principles of learning, growth, and development. I will begin by briefly describing the general process for implementing activities from a constructive perspective.

Guidelines for Conducting Reflective Activities

In articulating the use of structured activities for facilitating growth and change in clients, constructivist psychotherapists have cautioned practitioners not to become overly reliant on techniques at the expense of the more central elements of constructivist therapy (Neimeyer, 1995). As Mahoney (2006) stated, constructive psychotherapy "should be not be defined by techniques, but an overall conceptualization of human experience, knowing, and development" (p. 58). Mahoney considered techniques as another language that constructive psychotherapists could use to communicate their message with a broader range of people, but he cautioned practitioners not to "mistake the language for the message" (p. 58).

Like constructive psychotherapists, constructive supervisors use structured activities in ways that provide alternative means of allowing supervisees to discover their own answers in supervision. Consistent with the use of reflective questions and other constructive processes, this process of self-discovery is facilitated when supervisors provide supervisees with autonomy; facilitate supervisee creativity and self-reflection; and help them become comfortable with anxiety, change, and the unknown. Structured activities, therefore, are most successful when they are conducted in ways that honor the principles of human growth, change, and development that have been articulated throughout this book. Most essential to this process is for the focus of the activities to be on the meaning that supervisees make of the activities, not on the activities themselves (Neimeyer, 2009).

In addition to focusing on process and supervisee meaning making, the success of structured activities in clinical supervision is also dependent upon the extent to which supervisees endorse and willingly engage in the activities. From my experience, the way in which supervisors introduce and frame the activities is crucial in determining their success. Supervisors who are apprehensive when introducing activities or who impose activities on supervisees have far less chance of them authentically engaging in the activity than when supervisors introduce the activity confidently, while also providing supervisees with a legitimate choice about whether to participate. Activities should also be introduced using the same language described in the previous chapter for facilitating creativity and risk-taking in supervisees. The following is one example of how a supervisor can introduce an activity during supervision:

SUPERVISOR: You seem to be having difficulty making sense of this case. Rather than providing you with my answers, I believe it will be more helpful to you if we explore some more creative ways of helping develop your own answers.

SUPERVISEE: Okay, what do you have in mind?

SUPERVISOR: Well, sometimes when supervisees get stuck like this, it can be useful to try an activity to help you think more creatively about the client's issues. Would you like to try an experiment that might help you develop some news ways of thinking about the client's issues?

These directions are short and straightforward, but convey several important points about the proposed activity, which include: (1) a rationale for using the activity—to help supervisees develop their own answers, which the supervisor believes to be a more meaningful approach for them than simply providing them with an answer; (2) wording that suggests optimism for finding their own answers through participating in the activity, without promising any breakthroughs; (3) the word *experiment* to emphasize the tentative and creative nature of the activity; and (4) providing supervisees with the choice of whether or not to engage in the activity. While this sample introduction includes what I believe to be the necessary ingredients, constructive supervisors should experiment with alternative wording for introducing activities in ways that work for them and their supervisees.

Consistent with other elements of the constructive approach, constructive supervisors also approach the activities in a creative manner, which often means deviating from the established guidelines to adopt their use to unique situations. The directions presented to the supervisee for each activity should be thought of as general guidelines rather than something to which they should stringently adhere. The same activity, therefore, can and should look different with different supervisees. In this way, the activity itself becomes a co-constructed experiment that can be adapted in multiple ways depending upon any number of contextual factors. In the next section, I provide examples of several activities that can be particularly useful in facilitating supervisee growth and development from a constructive perspective.

Metaphoric Drawing Activities

Several authors have suggested that metaphoric drawing activities can help supervisees synthesize complex cognitive, behavioral, emotional, and interpersonal information to arrive at new conclusions or levels of awareness (Amundson, 1988; Guiffrida, Jordan, Saiz, & Barnes, 2007). These activities can be especially useful for supervisees who are artistically inclined; however, drawing activities can be adapted and useful for supervisees of any level of artistic ability (Guiffrida et al. 2007). Below I will describe two metaphoric drawing activities that can be particularly useful in assisting supervisees in thinking creatively about their cases:

metaphoric case drawing (Ishiyama, 1988; Stone & Amundson, 1989) and "Where am I?" (Saiz & Guiffrida, 2001).

Metaphoric Case Drawing

The first metaphoric drawing activity that is useful for facilitating supervisee case conceptualization skills in both individual and small group clinical supervision is metaphoric case drawing, which has been described and studied by both Ishiyama (1988) and Stone and Amundson (1989). Below, I will summarize ways of conducting the activity as presented by Ishiyama (1988).

To begin, the supervisor asks the supervisees to reflect, in writing, about a specific counseling session or case with which they are having difficulty conceptualizing. These reflections can be done during the supervision session or supervisees can be asked to complete this writing task outside of the session and to come to supervision prepared to discuss their reflections. To assist supervisees in this reflective process, Ishiyama suggested that supervisors ask their supervisees to complete, in writing, the following six sentence stems:

- What I see as the client's main concern is . . .
- The way the client interacted with me is . . .
- What I was trying to do in this session is . . .
- What I felt or thought about myself as a counselor in this session is . . .
- The way the session went is . . .
- What I think the client gained from the session is . . .

After writing their responses to these six sentence stems, supervisees are then asked to respond, in writing, to a second set of sentence stems that are designed to encourage case conceptualization through metaphoric thinking:

- The way I perceived the client with his or her concern may be characterized by a metaphor or an image like . . .
- The way the client responded to me and felt toward me during this session may be characterized by a metaphor or an image like . . .
- The way I conducted myself during this session may be characterized by a metaphor or image like . . .
- The way this session went may be characterized by a metaphor or image like . . . (p. 156).

Next, supervisees are asked to illustrate the case by drawing it using metaphoric images and symbols and then to present the drawing to the supervisor and the other supervisees (if done in a small group). Supervisees should be encouraged to be creative in their drawings and not to feel inhibited should they perceive themselves as lacking artistic ability. Supervisees who appear especially uncomfortable with drawing can be encouraged to bring in artwork from other sources that they feel represents their thinking about the client, such as books, magazines, or online materials.

As supervisees present their drawings or artwork, the supervisor and the group members are encouraged to assist the supervisee in his or her case conceptualization by asking questions, expressing empathic understanding of the issues, and extending the presenter's metaphor. After the discussion, supervisees can be encouraged to discuss their responses to the questions that arise from the supervisor and other group members and to change or adapt the drawing to reflect the new insight that occurred as a result of the discussion. Additionally, supervisees can decide to share their drawings with their clients to generate discussions about client issues or the counselor/client relationship.

Results of two separate studies have supported the efficacy of this metaphoric drawing activity in facilitating case conceptualization skills in supervisees. In the first study, Ishiyma (1988) found that thirteen of the nineteen supervisees in the study rated the metaphoric drawing activity to be superior to a non-visual method in encouraging them to conceptualize their client issues deeply and develop interventions. Additionally, qualitative data collected as part of the same study suggested that the metaphoric drawing activity was particularly helpful to students who were visual learners or who preferred an artistic medium of expression.

In another study, Stone and Amundson (1989) compared a similar metaphoric drawing technique to traditional verbal case debriefing with seven counselor interns at a community crisis center. They found greater gains from the metaphor group in the five areas related to counselor development (addressing concerns of clients, the development of the counselor, the client/counselor relationship, the counselor goals, and the perceived value of supervision) when compared to supervisees who were supervised using the traditional supervision method. The results also revealed that the metaphoric drawing group met an average 20 percent less with their supervisors, which suggested the technique might have been more efficient than the traditional verbal method. Moreover, the analysis revealed that the supervisees using the metaphoric drawing method tended to present more emotionally charged cases (i.e., suicide, depression, relationship conflicts) and frustrating cases (i.e., chronic clients) than those in the verbal supervision group. While both studies were limited by small sample sizes and lack of extensive controls, the results support the use of metaphoric drawing activities in facilitating supervisee case conceptualization skills.

Where Am I?

A second metaphoric drawing activity that can be useful to facilitate supervisee case conceptualization skills is called "Where am I?" (Saiz & Guiffrida, 2001). To begin this activity, the supervisor draws a stick figure on a piece of blank paper to represent the supervisee's client. The supervisor then asks the supervisee to place an "X" on the paper where she feels she is in relation to the client. The supervisor explains that the "X" can appear above the client, below the client, on either side of the client, or any other plane that the supervisee feels would accurately describe the context of her relationship with the client.

Next, the supervisor assists the supervisee in exploring and understanding why the supervisee placed the X on that particular space. The supervisor begins by asking the supervisee to use a metaphor to describe what it is like to be in the spot they indicated on their drawing. Examples of metaphoric responses to this question include "It is like carrying a heavy load on my shoulders" or "I feel like the client is weighing me down." If the supervisee experiences difficulty formulating a metaphoric response to the question, the supervisor can assist by asking a series of follow-up questions relative to the supervisee's position. For example, if supervisees draw themselves above the client, the supervisor would ask if it feels as if they are teaching or directing the client or if they feel they are superior in some way to the client. Supervisees placing themselves below the client could be prodded to explore if they feel like they are carrying or supporting the client or to investigate if they somehow feel inferior or unworthy of the client. Supervisees who place themselves behind the client could be asked if they feel they are pushing the client or if they are having a hard time keeping up with the client.

Once the supervisee develops a metaphor to describe the relationship with the client, the supervisor helps the supervisee expand the metaphoric image by asking questions designed to facilitate an understanding of sensory images related to her work with the client. To begin, the supervisor asks the supervisee to expand her metaphoric image. For example, the supervisor could ask questions geared toward exploring the visual (e.g., What do you see when you think about yourself being below this client?) or auditory (e.g., What sounds do you notice?) sensations experienced while immersed in the metaphoric image. Questions regarding affective and cognitive reactions found in the metaphor (e.g., What feelings or thoughts surround you in the metaphor?) can also be used. In order to help the supervisee understand how systemic and contextual factors affect the client's situation, the supervisor can use questions such as "Who else is involved in the metaphor?" and "Where might you place these other people in relation to yourself and the client?" Additionally, the supervisor can also use the metaphoric image to explore the supervisee's perceptions of her client's experience in the metaphor by asking, "How do you think your client feels about you being positioned below him/her in the relationship?"

Finally, the supervisor invites the supervisee to change the metaphor in any way she feels necessary to better assist the client by asking, "If you could make some change to the metaphor, what might it be?" After the supervisee elaborates on the various components of the metaphoric image, the supervisor asks the supervisee to use the metaphor to assist her in: (1) understanding her relationship with the client; (2) formulating a new conceptualization of the client's issues; and (3) recognizing how the metaphor, and the changes she made to the metaphor, can inform her future directions with her client.

While the activity was originally designed to facilitate case conceptualization skills with supervisees who are early in their clinical experiences (Saiz & Guiffrida, 2001), I have found that the activity can be effectively used with supervisees from any developmental level who are struggling with case conceptualization or therapeutic relationship issues. I have even used the activity with beginning supervisors who are struggling to conceptualize their work with their supervisees. The following is one example of how the activity was used to facilitate case conceptualization with a beginning counselor supervisor.

Cindy, an experienced counselor who was a new counselor supervisor, expressed frustration in helping her supervisee conceptualize her client issues in a deep manner. To assist her in understanding this dynamic, I invited her to participate in the "Where am I?" activity described above, but to draw herself in relationship to the supervisee and the supervisee's client. In her drawing, Cindy located the client directly between the supervisor and the supervisee. When asked why she chose this positioning, she explained that she perceived herself and the supervisee to have focused intensively on the client; this intense focus on the client was highlighted by the fact that she then drew one-way arrows pointing from the supervisee to the client and from herself to the client (even though she had no direct contact with the client).

In processing the meaning behind her positioning of the supervisor, supervisee, and client and her arrows between them, Cindy described how both she and the supervisee had invested most of their time and energy during supervision mutually brainstorming about the client's possible diagnosis and the underlying causes of the client's problem. They had not, however, focused on other dimensions of clinical supervision, including the counselor/client and supervisee/supervisor relationships or the supervisee's personalization of the case. When provided additional time and space to process the meaning that she made of the activity with her supervisor, Cindy decided that this intensive focus on helping the supervisee diagnose the client was limiting her ability to form a meaningful relationship with her supervisee and was not providing the supervisee with conditions that allowed her to creatively conceptualize the case. Moreover, Cindy hypothesized that the strong focus on client diagnosis actually served to keep both her and the supervisee "safe" by keeping them from considering the potentially deeper behaviors, thoughts, feelings, etc. of the supervisee.

Ultimately, Cindy's analysis of her drawing helped her to discover a parallel process that was occurring. She noticed that the supervisee had displayed an intense focus on diagnosis during her counseling session and she hypothesized that this focus was serving to keep the supervisee "safe" by preventing her from exploring more of the client's affective components. This same focus on diagnosis was also occurring in supervision as a way of protecting both the supervisee and the supervisor from experiencing emotional reactions during supervision. Armed with this insight, Cindy was able to gently encourage her supervisee to explore personalization issues, which included exploring her feelings about her client, and her strong reactions to and personal experiences with the client's presenting problem. The intervention also included exploring both the supervisee's and the supervisor's perceptions of the supervisory relationship. Eventually, Cindy shared with the supervisee that she too, as a new supervisor, was somewhat frightened by the idea of exploring potentially intense emotional issues with her supervisee because she was unsure about how to effectively balance the counselor role as a supervisor. The metaphoric drawing Cindy created, and the reflective processing that occurred as a result of the drawing, ultimately allowed Cindy to develop new hypotheses about why her supervisee remained "stuck" during supervision and to develop interventions that allowed the supervisee to explore new and more powerful dimensions of her client and herself.

Sand Tray

Another artistic activity that can be used in both individual and small group supervision to facilitate supervisee case conceptualization is the sand tray, which is a tool that has long been used to help children express and work through unconscious thoughts and feelings through play (Markos, Coker, & Jones, 2008). While the sand tray is most often used by supervisors of child therapists, since they are most likely to already be comfortable in using play as a modality in clinical supervision (and they may already have their own sand trays), it is an intervention that can be effective with a wide range of supervisees, including those who do not work with children (Markos et al., 2008).

Similar to the process of Sand Tray Therapy, use of the sand tray in supervision involves the supervisor offering various sand tray items, including storybook characters, animals, vehicles, and a small sandbox, and asking the supervisee to use the figures to depict themes, issues, and relationships in their clients' lives within the sand tray. Once they have finished creating their sand displays, supervisees are asked to describe their scenes with the supervisor and, if done in a small group, the other supervisees. Supervisors can also ask supervisees to take a picture of the sand tray as a way of documenting their thinking.

Consistent with the other activities described in this chapter, the characters the supervisee chooses and the placement of the characters are less important than the meaning the supervisee makes of the scene. Similar to the metaphoric drawing activity, the role of the supervisor and other supervisees (if conducted in a small group) is to demonstrate empathic understanding and to ask questions to help the supervisee clarify particular elements of the scene. Supervisees are then encouraged to discuss their responses to the questions that arise from the supervisor and other group members and to change or adapt their scene to reflect any new insights that may have occurred as a result of the discussion. Supervisees can also be asked to place themselves in relation to their clients in the sand using one of the sand items and to (1) describe why they chose a particular character to represent themselves and (2) why they placed it in a particular location in the sand. Once again, supervisees can take a picture of this second scene as a means of documenting their updated thinking about a case.

After describing and altering their original scene, Markos et al. (2008) suggest that it can be useful to ask supervisees to adapt the scene once more to depict changes they would like to see in their client's life, or possible outcomes as a result of therapy. This last adaptation can depict possible intervention strategies that might help facilitate these client outcomes. These final sand tray scenes can also be photographed to document the evolution of their case conceptualizations.

To further illustrate the process of sand tray supervision and to illuminate the ways in which the activity can facilitate case conceptualization skills in supervisee, I will briefly summarize one case example that was described by Markos et al. (2008). After receiving the instructions from the supervisor, the supervisee in Markos et al.'s study began the activity by creating two large mountains of sand: one depicting the client's home life, and the other depicting his classroom life. The supervisee then carefully selected characters to depict her client, his family members, teacher, and the other children who had been affected by his problematic behavior (bullying). As she selected each character, she described her rationale for selecting each one based on particular characteristics of each person that were described by the client. The supervisee then moved the mountains farther apart to depict the wide gap she perceived between the client's home and school lives.

After completing the scene, the supervisor then asked the supervisee to provide an overall depiction of the scene and to describe her thoughts and emotions about the scene she had created. The supervisee began by describing her frustration with the client's teacher and the control the teacher tried to exert over the student. She also spoke about the widening gap between the client's home and school lives, feeling that home was a very safe and supportive place for the client, while school was controlling and unsafe.

Next the supervisee was asked to adapt the scene to depict changes she hoped to see in the client's life. She responded by placing a bridge between the clients home and school lives (depicted by two lumps of sand); moved the client's uncle, who she had described as very supportive of the client, closer to the school mountain; and moved the figure depicting herself closer to the teacher to represent her more active involvement with and advocacy for the client in school. Most importantly, she then described specific intervention procedures she would need to enact to accomplish these goals, which included contacting the client's mother to set up a meeting, requesting to meet with other school support staff regarding her concerns about the teacher, and investigating developmental guidance programs to help reduce the client's problematic behavior with other children. The supervisee in Markos et al.'s study then translated the story she created in the sand into a formal conceptualization of the case and objectives for future sessions.

Markos et al. (2008) conducted a small pilot study with six supervisees that supported the efficacy of the sand tray in clinical supervision. Overall, supervisees rated the sand tray supervision slightly higher than traditional supervision modalities. Additionally, the study included qualitative data in which they documented the creative processes that supervisees engaged in while participating in sand tray supervision. The authors concluded that the kinesthetic and visual representations created in the sand tray helped the supervisees conceptualize their cases in new and creative ways to establish a vision for change that may have been previously unavailable to them. The sand tray also appeared to facilitate supervisees' understandings of their personal and emotional reactions to particular cases.

Reflective Writing Activities

Another activity that can be used in both individual and small group supervision to facilitate critical self-reflection in supervisees is reflective writing. From a constructivist perspective, writing can be especially useful in assisting people in organizing confusing or conflicting thoughts and feelings in order to develop new understandings. In this sense, one does not engage in writing to report what one knows, but rather to figure out what it is one knows. When framed from this exploratory perspective, writing can serve as a powerful tool in allowing supervisees to critically reflect upon their experiences and develop new knowledge about their clients, the therapeutic process, and themselves. Below I provide two examples of reflective writing activities that can be particularly useful during clinical supervision: therapeutic letter writing and reflective journals.

Therapeutic Letter Writing

While therapists have long used letters to clients as part of the therapeutic process (Pearson, 1965), the popularity of therapeutic letter writing as a clinical intervention greatly expanded with the rise of narrative therapy, which explicitly incorporates letters from therapists to clients as part of the therapeutic process (White & Epston, 1990). In the letters, narrative therapists summarize key themes that have arisen during therapy to highlight their understanding of the clients' problems, underscore progress clients have made during therapy, and encourage them to continue their process of self-exploration. The process is specifically designed to demonstrate therapist support for the client and to reinforce gains they have made during therapy, which, from a narrative perspective, are recognized through learning to externalize problems and re-author their problematic life narratives.

Research suggests that clients often perceive therapeutic letters as highly meaningful, some even rating the letters as more effective in facilitating change than their actual face-to-face sessions with therapists (Nylund & Thomas, 1994). However, in addition to therapeutic letters being helpful to clients, the therapeutic letter writing process can also assist counselors in articulating their clinical assessments about clients, discerning potential intervention strategies, and understanding their feelings toward their clients. For these reasons, therapeutic letter writing can be a useful activity to use during supervision, even if supervisees do not actually give the letters to their clients.

Supervisors seeking to implement this activity as part of the clinical supervision process can begin by discussing the potential benefits of the activity with supervisees. Supervisors should also inform supervisees that they are not required to give the letters to their clients, but that sharing the letters with clients is a possibility if they and the supervisor decide the letters would be beneficial to clients.[1] Supervisees who agree to participate are invited to write a brief (two to three page) letter to their client (typically written outside of the supervision session) in which they highlight their understanding of the client's issues or concerns and themes that emerged for them during their session. It is important to highlight that this letter is written *to* the client, not *about* the client. As such, the letters need to be written in a way that their clients can easily understand, which means refraining from the use of psychotherapeutic jargon. Supervisees should also honestly, but as compassionately as possible, describe the thoughts and emotions that they experienced as they heard their clients share their stories with them.

After articulating their understanding of the client issues and their cognitive and emotional reactions to the client, supervisees should then briefly pose questions to the client that remain unclear to them. In the letter, they can also articulate their reasons for wanting to ask these questions. Supervisees are instructed to conclude their letters by stating to clients the things they hope to accomplish with them and the steps they plan to take, as therapists, to accomplish these goals. Upon completing the letters, supervisees can be invited to share their letters with the supervisor and other supervisees (if conducted in small group supervision) and engage in a dialogue about learning that occurred for them as a result of authoring the letter.

Another variation of therapeutic letter writing that can be easily adapted for use in clinical supervision is when therapists ask clients to write letters to themselves in the future (White & Epson, 1990), which is often focused on a time soon after they have successfully completed therapy. This activity can be useful in facilitating hope in clients who are discouraged or overwhelmed by their problems and to inspire creative problem solving (Kress, Hoffman, & Thomas, 2008). Supervisors wishing to implement this activity with supervisees who are also experiencing discouragement with their progress with clients or their own development as counselors can ask their supervisees, usually after their first or second supervision session, to write a letter to themselves from their future self about their successful completion of the clinical supervision experience. Specifically, they can be asked to write about the specific behaviors, internal resources, or outside sources of support that helped them overcome challenges they encountered with their clients and during supervision. They can also be asked to articulate the things that their supervisor provided that allowed them to successfully navigate the experience. In addition to providing hope and encouragement to supervisees, the letters can also be used to help supervisors understand supervisee fears, hopes, and expectations of them and can serve as a springboard for discussing these issues during clinical supervision. Supervisors may also choose to save the letters and introduce them at the completion of the supervision experience as a means of highlighting supervisee growth.

Reflective Journals

Another activity that can help supervisees reflect upon their counseling experiences is reflective journaling, which encourages supervisees to formally reflect on their experiences outside of the supervision session. There are numerous ways in which reflective journaling can occur in supervision depending upon the writing interests, abilities, and backgrounds of the supervisees. Some options include asking supervisees to keep daily or weekly reflections of their experiences with clients, to develop reflective lists each week about their practice (e.g., things that I like or dislike about my clients, things that confuse me about my clients), or to write poems or short stories about their clients or their experiences in psychotherapy or supervision.

Another more formalized option for integrating reflective journaling into clinical supervision is the *Critical Incident Analysis*. This is an activity that was originally developed by teacher educators (Francis, 1995) to facilitate reflective thinking in pre-service teachers, but I have adapted it for use with counselors in clinical supervision. To begin the activity, supervisees are instructed to write a brief description of a dilemma they encountered during one of their counseling sessions. Supervisees should be instructed to describe the details of the event using rich and thick descriptions, and to refrain from making judgments at this point about any aspect of the dilemma. Consistent with the ideas expressed by John Dewey (1938) regarding learning from experience, the intent of this judgment-free, thick, written description is to help supervisees temporarily suspend their automatic assumptions and reactions to more fully understand all aspects of the dilemma. Supervisees should also reflect on the meaning they are making of the dilemma, which includes describing all feelings and thoughts associated with the event. Next supervisees can be encouraged to make a comparison between the current dilemma and some other dilemma they may have faced in their past. This can assist them in understanding the origins of their assumptions about the current dilemma, as well as allow them to draw from knowledge developed from prior experiences. They conclude this portion of the reflective writing activity by developing a list of questions that remain for them as they attempt to better understand all facets of the current dilemma.

After completing the reflective journal, supervisees are instructed to share their reflections with their supervisor (if done in individual supervision) or with their other supervisees (if done in small group supervision). The role of the supervisor and other group members is to help the supervisee generate new understandings of the dilemma and to begin formulating ways of addressing the issue based on these new understandings. After discussing this issue in detail with the supervisor/group members, supervisees are then instructed to summarize, either in writing or verbally, any new insights they have developed as a result of the reflective exercise and to describe additional questions that have arisen for them as a result of the writing activity and subsequent discussion. They can also be instructed, as a follow-up assignment, to detail their tentative plans for addressing the issue and to critically deconstruct these plans in writing using the same reflective processes.

Neufeldt (1999) has presented another reflective writing activity designed to encourage supervisees to use reflective processes to understand and learn from dilemmas they encounter during their counseling sessions. Unlike the reflective writing activity described above, Neufeldt's reflective writing activity is designed to enable supervisees to engage in this reflective process on their own outside of scheduled supervision session. As such, Neufeldt has developed a much more detailed and thorough list of questions for supervisees to respond to in writing. The questions/statements include the following:

- Describe the therapy events that precipitated your puzzlement.
- State your question about these events as clearly as you can.
- What were you thinking during this portion of the session?
- What were you feeling? How do you understand those feelings now?
- Consider your own actions during this portion of the session. What did you intend?
- Now look at the interaction between you and the client. What were the results of your intervention?
- What was the feel, the emotional flavor, of the interaction between you? Was it similar to or different from your usual experience with this client?
- To what degree do you understand this interaction as similar to the clients' interactions in other relationships? How does that inform your experience of the interaction in session?
- What theories do you use to understand what is going on in session?
- What past professional or personal experiences affect your understandings?
- How else might you interpret the events and interaction in the session?
- How might you test out the various alternatives in your next counseling session? (Be sure to look for what confirms and what disconfirms your interpretations.)
- How will the clients' responses inform what you do next? (p. 101)

Depending upon the supervisee's comfort and experience with writing, it can take a considerable amount of time for supervisees to answer each question in a meaningful way. Neufeldt has asserted, however, that the process can help supervisees establish a "habit" (p. 101) of reflective thinking about their cases that may carry on long past the current supervision experience. After completing the written assignments, supervisors may ask supervisees to submit their responses to them so the supervisor can review the ways in which they are reflecting and gain insight into their thought processes. Supervisors could also ask supervisees to come to supervision prepared to provide the supervisor and group members with a summary of their responses to the questions and to describe the learning that occurred for them as a result of the activity.

While research has not tested the efficacy of reflective journals with supervisees in clinical supervision, research indicates that the activities can be beneficial in facilitating critical self-reflection in pre-service teachers. Specifically, Francis (1995) reported increased non-judgmental awareness of self and others among teaching students who participated in the *Critical Incident Analysis* reflective writing activity. While more research is needed to understand the effects of the activities in clinical supervision, anecdotal evidence suggests that reflective writing can be useful to supervisees who are struggling with self-reflection and in developing their own answers.

Client Facetime

Client Facetime is an activity that can assist supervisees in thinking more deeply about their relationship to their clients, to conceptualize their cases in new ways, or to meaningfully reflect on personalization issues that may be affecting their work. The activity is an adaptation of Mahoney's (1991) *Mirror Time* activity, which is a psychotherapy activity based on constructivist notions of growth and change. In *Mirror Time*, the counselor literally invites clients to reflect on themselves by placing a mirror in front of them and asking them to gently reflect, either silently or verbally to the counselor, on their thoughts, feelings, and self-perceptions as they look closely at themselves in the mirror. In addition to being used as a tool for general client self-exploration, the activity has also been used to assist clients with specific self-conceptualization issues, including body image and self-esteem issues.

In his book *Human Change Processes,* Mahoney (1991) shared how he discovered this activity serendipitously. One day a client arrived for counseling with a mirror that he presented to Mahoney as a gift. The client had won the mirror at a local festival over the weekend and wanted to give it to him because it was inscribed with a logo that reminded him of his counselor. Later that day, another client noticed the addition of this mirror to the office and commented that seeing his reflection in it was distracting and made him feel uncomfortable. He then asked Mahoney to move the mirror. In true constructivist fashion, Mahoney, as an experiment, placed the mirror directly in front of the client and asked him to describe what he saw. Although the client initially resisted the exercise, he ended up, in a later session, asking if he could look into the mirror again and describe to the counselor what he saw. This time, the activity proved meaningful to the client as he shared detailed thoughts and feelings about himself, while also gaining tremendous insight regarding the origins of these self-perceptions. Armed with this success with one client, Mahoney began experimenting with the activity with other clients and eventually conducted several studies to examine the efficacy of the activity with a broader range of clients.

Research suggests that clients participating in the mirror activity showed increases in psychological arousal and self-focus during the activity, suggesting that the activity initiated active self-reflection (Beskow & Palm, 1998; Williams, Diehl, & Mahoney, 2002). Additionally, qualitative data collected by Williams et al.

(2002) indicated that many of the participants engaged in deep, meaningful reflections, both during the activity and during post-activity reflection time. Participants referred to their reflections as both positive and unpredictable, meaning that they reflected on themselves in ways that they had not anticipated. Interestingly, participants reported being especially reflective during the post-mirror stage of the experiment when they processed with the researcher their feelings about the experience with the mirror. This finding suggests that mirror time alone is not sufficient to fully capitalize on the reflective processes inherent in the activity and that additional processing of the activity should occur afterwards.

Williams et al. (2002) also compared how participants reacted to two different formats of the *Mirror Time* activity: one in which participants were not provided with any guidance from the researcher, and another where they were provided with comments and questions from the researcher to prompt their reflective thinking. The questions/statements, which were played for them on an audio recording, included the following:

- Pay attention to how you are feeling while seeing yourself in the mirror.
- Notice any thoughts or feelings you may have and know that they are just part of the process of this time you are spending.
- If you could divide yourself into a questioning part and an answering part, what might you ask?
- Do you sense a response?
- What might you say to yourself that would be caring?

Interestingly, results comparing the researcher-guided reflection versus non-guided client reflection were mixed. While some participants found that the researcher statements and questions greatly enhanced their reflective processing, others described them as distracting and indicated that they would have preferred to have reflected on their own without comments and questions from the researchers. The researchers were unable to discern any noticeable differences between those who preferred the guided reflections and those who did not, and thus concluded that the process should be done in a flexible way that allows the counselor to explore which format (open-ended or guided questions) fits best with each client.

Client Facetime provides an opportunity to harness the reflective power of this constructivist psychotherapy activity with supervisees during clinical supervision. Rather than asking supervisees to look at themselves in a mirror, supervisors conducting this activity ask supervisees to engage in this same reflective practice while looking at a video still photo of their clients. Like most constructivist activities, this activity works best when it is approached in a spontaneous, free flowing, and experimental way. In other words, rather than formally planning to conduct the activity and introducing it with a long series of instructions, supervisors can initiate it at any time they are watching a videotaped session with their supervisee and an impasse arises. The activity begins with the supervisor asking the supervisee to find a section on their counseling video where they can see the client's face clearly on the screen and to pause it at that spot. The supervisor can then ask the supervisee to respond to the following questions, while closely examining the paused video of their client's face:

- Gently observe what you notice as you look at the client. What are you thinking and feeling as you look at her/him now?
- What does the expression on the client's face tell you about how he or she is feeling at the moment in the session when you paused the tape?
- Look deeply into the client's eyes. What do you see?
- What do you like or dislike about this client?
- Does this client remind you of anyone?

After the supervisee completes this series of questions, the supervisor can then ask the supervisee to close her eyes, breathe deeply, and invite herself to become open to new possibilities of viewing her client and her relationship to her client. This aspect of the activity, which is likened to the post-mirror reflection time in the psychotherapy version of the activity, can be particularly useful in opening a dialogue in which the supervisee compares and contrasts her current understandings of her client with new, alternative ways of approaching the client in future sessions.

While the questions listed above can provide a starting point for helping supervisors initiate this activity, supervisors should feel free to omit questions that seem less meaningful for this particular situation and to insert their own questions. Additionally, supervisors may also want to experiment with a less structured and more free-flowing approach with some supervisees: instead of asking questions, they may choose to simply provide an overview of the activity and allow supervisees to freely explore whatever comes to mind while looking at the client. They could then be asked to share their reflections at a later time with the counselor, either in person or in writing. This recommendation is based upon Williams et al.'s (2002) findings with the *Mirror Time* activity that indicated that different clients preferred varying levels of counselor guidance to optimally facilitate their reflective thinking.

Mindfulness-Based Activities

As described in Chapter 2, teaching supervisees about mindfulness, specifically about how to be more present during counseling sessions, can improve supervisee listening skills and abilities to demonstrate empathy with clients (Grepmair, Mitterlehner, Loew, Bachler, Rother, & Nickel, 2007). Additionally, supervisees who learn to non-judgmentally observe themselves and their own practice often feel more relaxed when dealing with difficult client issues and can be more accepting of supervisor feedback (Christopher & Maris, 2010; Schure, Christopher & Christopher, 2008; Rothaupt & Morgan, 2007; Ryback & Russel-Chapin, 1998). Mindfulness, therefore, can be a valuable construct to introduce during clinical supervision.

As described in Chapter 2, supervisors integrating mindfulness into supervision begin by teaching supervisees the core elements of mindfulness. This can be done directly during supervision and by asking supervisees to read literature describing the basic elements of mindfulness and mindful counseling (see Chapter 2 for suggested readings). For some supervisees, learning about the basic mindfulness concepts may be enough for them to become more present, open, and reflective during therapy and supervision. Others, however, may struggle becoming mindful, even if the concepts of mindfulness resonate conceptually with them. In these cases, supervisors can offer to integrate some basic mindfulness-based exercises into supervision. While there are numerous mindfulness activities available (see Kabat-Zinn, 1994), three that are particularly useful during supervision are mindful breathing, lovingkindness meditation, and mindful eating. These three activities are brief (can be done in less than five minutes) and lend themselves easily to discussions about clinical practice. Below I provide details regarding how supervisors can integrate these mindfulness-based activities into clinical supervision to assist both supervisees and supervisors in being more open, present, and reflective.

Mindful Breathing

From a Buddhist perspective, the breath is sacred in its ability to connect the mind, body, and spirit. For this reason, the breath often serves as the center of mindfulness exercises. Mindful breathing is a simple, brief activity that can be used during supervision to help ground supervisees in the present moment. In this activity, supervisees are asked to sit quietly for as little as five minutes to consciously observe their own breath. To begin observing their breath, supervisees should be instructed to sit in a position that is comfortable, but that ensures that their backs are straight and upright. They are then instructed to close their eyes and pay attention to their natural breathing process. This begins by recognizing the sensation of air moving against the nostrils and the backs of their throats as they inhale, to focusing on the rising and falling of the chest and abdomen with each breath. To facilitate this observation, it can be helpful to ask supervisees to place a hand on their stomachs so they can actually feel the stomach rise and fall with each breath. When thoughts arise, as they undoubtedly will, supervisees should be encouraged to simply notice and accept these thoughts and to allow them to gently pass without any reaction, like clouds that float by in the sky of their minds, and to bring their attention back to their breathing. In this sense, the breath serves as an *anchor* to keep them from being distracted by or reacting to their thoughts.

After a few moments of conscious attention to the breath, I find it helpful to encourage supervisees to briefly allow themselves to non-judgmentally observe things from their day that might still be with them as they enter the supervision experience, or to allow them to actively recognize the things they might be in a hurry to get to after the supervision session is over. While doing this, they should be encouraged to gently observe and accept any reactions that might arise with them as they recognize these thoughts, worries, future plans, etc. At the end of the activity, I encourage them to consciously place these thoughts aside so that they can focus more intensively on the supervision session, recognizing that they can make time later to continue their planning or worrying.

This seemingly simple act of sitting and paying attention to one's own breath and observing, non-judgmentally, one's own thoughts, including the baggage both supervisee and supervisor may bring with them to the session, can help both the supervisee and the supervisor focus more intensively in the present moment and to be more accepting of all their thoughts and emotions. Beginning a session with this brief activity can, therefore, enhance the productivity of the supervision session. Initially, it can also be useful for the supervisor to invite the supervisee to share their experiences during this brief activity. This sharing can lead to insightful discussions about a range of issues that may be impacting their work with clients and their perceptions of the supervision experience, including their thoughts about their clients, anxiety about supervision, or things going on in their personal lives that may impact their experiences in supervision and as therapists.

Once supervisees become familiar with the basic process of mindful breathing, there may not be a need to process each experience of the brief meditation together. Mindful breathing can then become a five-minute activity that supervisors and supervisees mutually engage in at the beginning of every supervision session as a means of becoming more focused and present during supervision. However, the same type of purposeful attention can be used to assist supervisees in being more present to their thoughts, emotions, and physical sensations during other times of the supervision session. One way in which this can occur is for the supervisor to periodically provide supervisees with the opportunity to check in with their thoughts and emotions during the process of supervision, especially during times when supervisees seem particularly troubled. The supervisor might ask, for example, "As you are talking about your difficulty addressing the needs of your client, what thoughts go through you mind?" "What emotions are you feeling as we discuss this?" The supervisor might even ask the supervisee to reengage in the mindful breathing activity and to pay attention to the sensations the supervisee feels in his or her body as he or she conducts the exercise. At the same time, the supervisor is encouraging the supervisee to fully accept all the thoughts and feelings she or he may experience during this process, even those that may seem harsh or negative of themselves, their clients, or even the supervisor. Through this process, the supervisee learns that these thoughts are not reality, but just a perspective they have at that time that must be acknowledged and understood.

In my experience of leading this activity in classes, workshops, and in individual and small group supervision, I have noticed some patterns in how people react. Many people will describe the experience as initially uncomfortable, which will likely be evident by the amount of fidgeting they do as they attempt to settle in to the activity. When this occurs, it is useful to encourage supervisees to sit with and observe, as best they can, whatever minor physical discomfort they are experiencing without physically reacting to it. This is not to say that fidgeting or scratching is forbidden during the activity (insisting that people fight their urges only gives the urges more power); rather, I encourage them to reframe this as an experiment in which they simply try watching to see what happens when they do not initially fidget or scratch their itch. Many people are often surprised to see the discomfort go away once they focus their non-judgmental awareness on it.

Other people learning to experience mindful breathing for the first time will quickly fall asleep, or spend the entire time trying intensely to stay awake. This tends to be people who are not only sleep deprived, but who also experience very little quiet time in their lives. These folks tend to be the ones who begin the day going at full speed from the moment they get out of bed and go very hard (both physically and in their own minds) right up until they pass out at night. I often encourage these *sleepers* to actively seek moments of quiet during their day, which can begin with something as simple as spending their first five minutes of the day noticing their thoughts rather than jumping immediately into their daily activities. For others, it may mean challenging themselves to spend a few minutes of non-judgmental awareness of their thoughts before they fall asleep instead of falling asleep to the television.

While the fidgeters and sleepers constitute the largest percentage of responses to the initial mindfulness meditation activity described above, there is a smaller group of people who emerge from their first mindful breathing activity feeling refreshed, energized, and clear in thought. This is an outcome that some refer to as *falling awake*. These are the supervisees who are most likely to enthusiastically embrace mindful breathing and other mindfulness activities as a regular part of the supervision process and many will even continue meditation practices on their own.

Consistent with other aspects of the constructive approach, mindful breathing is not an activity that will be effective if it is perceived by supervisees as being forced on them. From my experience, however, most supervisees, even those who initially experience discomfort with the activity, often remain open to briefly practicing it each week when it is framed as an exercise that can help them improve their work with clients and be more focused and open during supervision. I have even framed it as something that is helpful in allowing me, as the supervisor, to be more focused and attentive to their needs during supervision, and asked that they indulge me by participating while I do it. In any event, most supervisees, with practice, can become more comfortable with the mindful breathing activity and this comfort often translates to being more mindful during supervision.

Lovingkindness/Compassion Meditation

Lovingkindness and compassion are two of the four divine abodes (along with sympathetic joy and equanimity) described by the Buddha for opening the heart and facilitating mindfulness. One way in which lovingkindness and compassion can be nurtured is through a brief meditation activity referred to as lovingkindness meditation. This activity, which has been used for over 2,000 years, has recently been adapted for use with clients in psychotherapy. In their review of research that has examined the efficacy of lovingkindness meditation in psychotherapy, Hoffman, Grossman, and Hinton (2011) concluded that the activity appears to promote positive affect in clients, can reduce subjective distress and corresponding immune responses, and enhances the activation of brain areas involved in emotional processing. Additionally, Kabat-Zinn (2005) has noted that lovingkindness meditation can "soften one's relationship" (p. 287) to strong emotions that can feel too overwhelming to non-judgmentally observe early in mindfulness practice. Thus, lovingkindness meditation can serve as a scaffold to help clients begin to recognize and experience thoughts and feelings they may have previously been unwilling or unable to access or accept.

In addition to serving as a counseling intervention, lovingkindness meditation is also something that can be used by clinical supervisors to facilitate supervisee development. Recall from Chapter 1 that developmental literature indicates that counselors from all developmental levels, from new students to seasoned professionals, can experience frustration and self-doubt. Self-doubt can be especially pervasive during counselors' early clinical experiences as they struggle to live up to their own expectations, prove their effectiveness to their supervisors and peers, and fix all of their clients. These developmental challenges can hinder the open and creative states that are needed for supervisees to benefit from clinical supervision and to flourish in their clinical practice. Lovingkindness meditation is an activity that supervisors can use to facilitate supervisee empathy toward clients and themselves, and to nurture creative processes during clinical supervision.

While there are numerous ways in which lovingkindness meditation can be introduced, most formats follow the same basic approach. To begin, participants are encouraged to focus on their breath and to have non-judgmental awareness of their thoughts and sensations, in the same way described in the mindful breathing activity. Once participants become grounded in observing their breath, they are encouraged to think of someone who loves them unconditionally. This can be a child, spouse, close friend, or even a pet. If participants are not able to immediately think of someone who matches these characteristics, they can be encouraged to imagine, as best as they can, what it would be like to have someone like that in their lives. As they continue to think about the person, participants are instructed to bask in the feelings of acceptance and unconditional love generated through this person. They are also encouraged to notice sensations in their bodies as they experience this unconditional feeling of love and acceptance. Participants are then encouraged to say to themselves, either in their own minds or quietly aloud, the following (from Kabat-Zinn, 2005, p. 289):

- May I be safe and protected and free from inner and outer harm.
- May I be happy and contented.
- May I be healthy and whole to whatever degree possible.
- May I experience ease of well-being.

Once participants begin to deeply experience this feeling of unconditional self-love and acceptance, they are then instructed to expand the field of lovingkindness to others. It is often easiest to have them begin by thinking of someone with whom they are already close. Once they begin thinking about this person, they are then encouraged to repeat the same statements to themselves that are listed above, but to insert the words "this person" instead of "I." Again, they should then be instructed to deeply experience and nurture this sense of lovingkindness as they repeat the statements.

If conducted as a psychotherapeutic intervention, clients would then be instructed to expand this same process to include others in their world, including people with whom they may have disagreements or hold negative feelings, and to even expand the process to include the entire planet. However, when conducting the activity with supervisees as part of a clinical supervision intervention, I have found it helpful to adapt this portion of the activity in a way that allows supervisees to focus directly on their clients at this point. Again, it can be helpful to scaffold the experience so that they begin focusing on a client with whom feelings of compassion and lovingkindness are easily experienced, and then engage in the same process with a client with whom they have thus far found it difficult to feel empathy. I have also found it helpful to adapt the self-statements in a way that captures outcomes that are more consistent with the supervisees' goals for their clients, rather than simply wishing broader positive outcomes on their clients such as health, safety, and happiness. The following provides one example of statements that could be used to help supervisors empathize with their supervisees:

- May my client feel heard and understood during our session.
- May my client feel completely safe to explore issues of meaning to her or him in our session.
- May my client be open to trying new things and take risks during our session.
- May my client feel empowered to make changes that he or she believes will improve her or his life.

In addition to facilitating empathy toward clients, this activity can also be adapted to develop and expand supervisee case conceptualization skills by changing some of the statements that they are asked to repeat to themselves. For example, instead of inserting already established goals for the supervisee to visualize, such as clients feeling more empowered, supervisors may ask the supervisees to insert their own goals for clients. Examples of this can include, "May my client feel [insert your own goal here] while they are with me," or "May my client begin to . . . as a result of our sessions together." These more open-ended statements, developed while feeling unconditional love and acceptance toward themselves and others, can allow supervisees to think about client outcomes in a new way by allowing them access to a more creative part of themselves. Supervisees can then be encouraged to share their thoughts with the supervisor and other supervisees (if done in a small group) to further develop the insights that arise as a result of the activity.

Mindful Eating

A third activity that can be easily integrated into a supervision session as a means of helping supervisees view their clients and themselves in a more open and non-judgmental way is mindful eating. It is also an activity that may initially seem more comfortable and familiar to supervisees than mindful breathing or loving-kindness meditation since eating is not something that is normally associated with formal meditation practice. While the focus of the activity is on eating, it is actually an activity that has been proven to increase participants' attention and reactive abilities immediately following their participation in mindful eating (Sugamura, Shiraishi, & Murakami, 2009).

After introducing the activity and explaining the rationale for doing it during supervision, the supervisor begins the activity by offering supervisees a box or plate of raisins and asking them to take three or four of them out and place them on a napkin or plate in front of them.[2] After they take their raisins, supervisees are then instructed to pick up one raisin and non-judgmentally focus their awareness on the sight and texture of the raisin, without placing the raisin in their mouths. After carefully examining the raisin for a minute or two, supervisees are asked to raise the raisin to their noses and focus intensively on the smell, while also continuing to observe the texture and sight of the raisin. After another minute or so, supervisees can then be instructed to gently place the raisin in their mouths, but to hold the raisin on their tongues so they can gently observe the feel of the raisin in their mouths. Finally, supervisees are instructed to slowly bite into the raisin and to non-judgmentally observe the flavors and textures of the raisin in their mouths as they gently chew it. As supervisees swallow, they are even encouraged to feel the raisin as it makes its way down their throats and into their stomachs. Throughout the activity, the supervisor reminds supervisees to notice when their attention has drifted away from their current experience to engage in other thoughts or judgments, and to return their attention to the physical experience of the raisin. Supervisees are then encouraged to continue the same process, on their own, with two or three additional raisins.

After supervisees mindfully eat all three or four raisins, they can then discuss their experiences of the activity with the supervisor and/or small group members. These conversations often begin with them stating they were able to taste the raisin in a new way by focusing intensively on the raisin and by removing their judgments about it. This can be particularly meaningful for participants who describe a prior distaste for raisins. The supervisor can then help relate their observations to the process of supervision by helping them explore their client and themselves in the same open, present, and non-judgmental way in which they observed the raisin. Therefore, in addition to facilitating a more present and less judgmental state that is conducive for supervision, the activity can also help supervisees to think more creatively about the processes of psychotherapy and clinical supervision.

Chapter Summary

In this chapter I have provided a number of activities that constructive supervisors can use to facilitate reflective thinking in supervisees. These activities can be particularly useful when supervisees experience difficulty or frustration in developing their own answers during clinical supervision. I have also provided guidelines for introducing the activities, for adapting the activities for use in both individual and small group supervision, and for engaging in the activities in ways that are consistent with constructivist principles of learning, growth, and development. It is important to highlight that the activities included in this chapter provide just a few examples of activities to consider when using the constructive approach. Many other possibilities exist. In the next section, I will describe the process of assessment in clinical supervision.

Notes

1 Supervisees deciding to share their letters with their clients should consult literature that details the use of therapeutic letters with clients, such as White and Epson (1990); Oliver, Nelson, Cade, and Cueva (2007); or Andrews, Clark, and Baird (1997).
2 In conducting this activity numerous times throughout the past couple of years, I found it helpful to allow participants to pick the raisins themselves rather than handing them out because many people to seem to be fearful of germ contamination when sharing food.

References

Amundson, N.E. (1988). The use of metaphor and drawings in case conceptualization. *Journal of Counseling and Development, 66*, 391–393.

Andrews, J., Clark, D.J., & Baird, F. (1997). Therapeutic letter writing: Creating relational case notes. *Family Journal: Counseling and Therapy for Couples and Families, 5*(2), 149–158.

Bernard, J.M., & Goodyear, R.K. (2014). *Fundamentals of clinical supervision*. Boston: Merrill.

Beskow, J., & Palm, A. (1998). The mirror technique. *Constructivism in the Human Sciences, 3*, 20–22.

Christopher, J.C., & Maris, J.A. (2010). Integrating mindfulness as self-care into counselling and psychotherapy training. *Counselling and Psychotherapy Research, 10*(2), 114–125.

Dewey, J. (1938). *Experience and education*. New York: Touchstone.

Francis, D. (1995). The reflective journal: A window to preservice teachers' practical knowledge. *Teaching and Teacher Education, 11*(3), 229–241.

Grepmair, L., Mitterlehner, F., Loew, T., Bachler, E., Rother, W. and Nickel, M. (2007). Promoting mindfulness in psychotherapists in training influences the treatment results of their patients: A randomized, double-blind, controlled study. *Psychotherapy and Psychosomatics, 76*(6), 332–338.

Guiffrida, D.A., Jordan, R.A., Saiz, S., & Barnes, K.L. (2007). Metaphor in supervision. *Journal of Counseling & Development, 85*, (4) 393–400.

Hofmann, S.G., Grossman, P., & Hinton, D.E. (2011). Loving-kindness and compassion meditation: Potential for psychological interventions. *Clinical Psychology Review, 31*(7), 1126–1132.

Ishiyama, F.I. (1988). A model of visual case processing using metaphors and drawings. *Counselor Education and Supervision, 28*, 153–161.

Kabat-Zinn, J. (1994). *Wherever you go there you are: Mindfulness meditation in everyday life.* New York: Hyperion.

Kabat-Zinn, J. (2005). *Full catastrophe living: How to cope with stress, pain and illness using mindfulness meditation.* New York: Random House.

Kress, V.E., Hoffman, R., & Thomas, A.M. (2008). Letters from the future: The use of therapeutic letter writing in counseling sexual abuse survivors. *Journal of Creativity in Mental Health, 3*(2), 105–118.

Mahoney, M.J. (1991). *Human change processes.* New York: Basic Books.

Mahoney, M.J. (2006). *Constructive psychotherapy: Theory and practice.* New York: Guilford.

Markos, P.A., Coker, J.K., & Jones, W.P. (2008). Play in supervision. *Journal of Creativity in Mental Health, 2*(3), 3–15.

Neimeyer, R.A. (1995). Constructivist psychotherapies: Features, foundations, and future directions. In R.A. Neimeyer & M.J. Mahoney (Eds.) *Constructivism in psychotherapy* (pp. 11–38). Washington, DC: American Psychological Association.

Neimeyer, R.A. (2009). *Constructivist psychotherapy: Distinctive features.* New York: Routledge.

Neufeldt, S.A. (1999). Training in reflective processes in supervision. In M. Carroll & E.L. Holloway (Eds.), *Education of Clinical Supervisors* (pp. 92–105). London: Sage.

Nylund, D., & Thomas, J. (1994). The economics of narrative. *The Family Therapy Networker, 18*(6), 38–39.

Oliver, M., Nelson, K.W., Cade, R., & Cueva, C. (2007). Therapeutic letter writing from school counselors to students, parents, and teachers. *Professional School Counseling, 10*(5), 510–515.

Pearson, L. (1965). *The use of written communications in psychotherapy.* Springfield, IL: Charles C. Thomas.

Rothaupt, J.W., & Morgan, M.M. (2007). Counselors' and counselor educators' practice of mindfulness: A qualitative inquiry. *Counseling and Values, 52*(1), 40–54.

Rybak, C.J. & Russell-Chapin, L.A. (1998). The teaching well: Experience, education, and counseling. *International Journal for the Advancement of Counseling, 20*, 131–139.

Saiz, S.G., & Guiffrida, D.A. (2001). *The use of metaphor in the supervision of counselor education students.* Paper presented at the North Atlantic Region of the Association for Counselor Education and Supervision's Annual Meeting: University of Massachusetts and Amherst, October.

Schure, M.B., Christopher, J., & Christopher, S. (2008). Mind–body medicine and the art of self-care: Teaching mindfulness to counseling students through yoga, meditation, and qigong. *Journal of Counseling & Development, 86*(1), 47–56.

Stone D., & Amundson, N. (1989). Counselor supervision: An exploratory study of the metaphoric case drawing method of case presentation in a clinical setting. *Counselor Supervision, 23*, 360–371.

Sugamura, G., Shiraishi, S., & Murakami, Y. (2009). Mindful eating enhances attention. *Health & Psychology, 24*, 378–379.

White, M., & Epston, D. (1990). *Narrative means to therapeutic ends.* New York: W.W. Norton.

Williams, A.M., Diehl, N.S., & Mahoney, M.J. (2002). Mirror-time: Empirical findings and implications for a constructivist psychotherapeutic technique. *Journal of Constructivist Psychology, 15*(1), 21–39.

5

ASSESSMENT

Assessment has been referred to as the "nucleus" of clinical supervision (Bernard & Goodyear, 2014, p. 222). It is listed as a primary supervisor responsibility in nearly every definition of clinical supervision and required by most professional organizations and licensing boards in the various helping professions. Yet despite the recognized importance of assessment to clinical supervision, it is also one of the most difficult and anxiety-provoking aspects for both supervisees and supervisors. In fact, Ladany, Lehrman-Waterman, Molinaro, and Wolgast (1999), in a study examining ethical complaints about supervisors, found that the vast majority of these complaints were regarding assessment practices.

One reason that counselor supervisors may find it difficult to assess supervisees is that assessment of clinical skills is the aspect of supervision that is most distinct from psychotherapy (Bernard & Goodyear, 2014). Clinical supervisors all began as psychotherapists who were trained to support clients rather than critique them. It is difficult for many psychotherapists, therefore, to point out supervisee limitations (Hoffman, Hill, Holmes, & Freitas 2005). Assessment is also complicated by the field's lack of agreement regarding the critical components of therapeutic competence and the lack of psychometrically sound assessment instruments (Ellis, D'Iuso, & Ladany, 2008). Assessment can seem even more difficult and confusing when supervising from an orientation based on constructivist principles of change and growth. After all, how can supervisors who endorse the existence of multiple realities and espouse a non-judgmental view of supervisee work provide a meaningful, authentic assessment of them?

In this chapter, I detail the process of supervisee assessment from a constructive perspective. I begin by providing an overview of constructivist principles of assessment, which are drawn largely from constructivist psychotherapy literature. In doing so, I delineate key differences between constructivist principles of assessment and those used in traditional, behaviorist approaches to assessment. Next, I provide a description of how constructivist principles of assessment can be integrated into the practice of constructive clinical supervision, which includes utilizing supervisee self-assessment procedures. I also discuss how these constructivist principles of assessment can be used in conjunction with more traditional forms of assessment, along with presenting an instrument that can be used to assess supervisee growth and development specifically from a constructive perspective. I conclude this chapter by providing suggestions on how to present difficult feedback to supervisees who require additional learning experiences to attain required competencies.

Constructivist Principles of Assessment

As detailed in Chapter 1, constructivists oppose the notion that knowable, observable truths exist that can be generalized. Rather, constructivists seek to understand and validate individual perceptions of reality and understand knowledge in context. This perspective about reality has tremendous implications for the ways in which constructivists view and conduct assessment. Far from an "anything goes" approach, constructivist psychotherapists and supervisors have adapted assessment procedures that allow nuanced assessments of clients and supervisees in ways that reflect local and contextualized forms of knowledge and that recognize humans as active agents who continually interpret and make meaning of their worlds.

In his book titled *Constructivist Assessment*, Neimeyer (1993) provided a detailed description of how constructivist principles of assessment can be utilized by psychotherapists to assess clients. He began by contrasting constructivist assessment principles with more traditional, behaviorist assessment practices. According to Neimeyer, many contemporary forms of psychotherapy assessment are based on behaviorist principles so this comparison allowed distinguishing features of constructivist assessment to emerge. Similarly, I will begin defining constructivist assessment principles in clinical supervision using the same comparison presented by Neimeyer.

To begin, Neimeyer (1993) asserted that behaviorists believe assessment procedures should be unobtrusive and not impact those being assessed. Constructivists, however, recognize that all forms of assessment reflect some form of intervention by encouraging clients and supervisees to rethink their own stances about what is being evaluated and how they make meaning of their lives. As Neimeyer (1993) stated, "From this perspective, assessment is inherently a change-providing process that can be harnessed and directed toward promoting personal reconstruction" (p. 12). Constructive supervisors, therefore, recognize that assessment procedures often assist supervisees in developing new awareness and understanding of themselves and their clients, and as a result, do not seek to compartmentalize or distinguish assessment from intervention procedures.

Second, behaviorist assessments in clinical supervision tend toward isolating particular elements of counseling activity (e.g., ability to ask open-ended questions, focus on feeling). Constructivists, however, place a greater emphasis on semantic holism, which Neimeyer (1993) defines as "the belief that any given construction can be best understood within the context of the broader system of meaning that supports it" (p. 13). One example is the ability to explore deep and painful emotions with clients. From a behaviorist perspective, supervisees are encouraged to engage in this behavior through supervisor teaching (e.g., how and when to ask feeling-oriented questions) and reinforcement (e.g., compliments and good ratings when they demonstrate the behavior and critiques and low ratings when they do not).

While constructive supervisors may also encourage supervisees to explore deep and painful emotions with clients, they also recognize that helping to facilitate meaningful changes in others requires much more than encouraging them to adopt a new behavior. Constructive supervisors, therefore, seek to examine and assess not only supervisee behavior, but also the thoughts, feelings, and contextual factors that may underlie the behavior. In the case of a supervisee having difficulty facilitating client exploration of emotions, constructive supervisors would seek to join with supervisees in understanding their resistances in addressing client emotional content. Is the resistance based on a fundamental assumption that emotions are not important in helping clients? If so, how did they develop these beliefs? Do they have a fear of dealing with strong client emotions? If so, are they afraid of all client emotions or is their fear limited only to one particular client or client issue? From this holistic perspective, supervisees are assessed not only on their behaviors, but also on their willingness to explore factors that underlie the behaviors.

A third difference highlighted by Neimeyer (1993) between traditional behaviorist assessment procedures and constructivist assessment principles relates to the notion of frequency. Behaviorist assessments typically focus on the number of times in which behaviors occur and these frequency counts provide baseline data from which to assess supervisee performance and improvement. For example, if a supervisee refrained from asking any feeling-oriented questions in his first counseling session, the objective for the next session, from a behavioral perspective, may be for him to ask at least two feeling-oriented questions. If the supervisee asked at least two feeling-oriented questions in his subsequent session, he would receive a favorable assessment. If he did not, he would receive a lower rating and be encouraged to increase his frequency of feeling-oriented questions in future sessions.

Constructivist supervisors would focus less on the frequency with which a particular behavior manifests and more on the contextual factors and the centrality of the behavior. Some sessions or particular segments of a supervisee's session may lend themselves more to the counselor introducing feeling-oriented questions than others. Likewise, supervisees may be conceptualizing client problems from a theoretical stance that does not prioritize client affective exploration. Constructivists would not find tallies of feeling-oriented questions in a session as helpful as being able to help supervisees identify and understand their rationale for

Behaviorist	Constructivist
Unobtrusive with minimal impact	Assessment is a form of intervention
Isolating particular elements and skills	Semantic holism
Frequency of behavior	Centrality of behavior
Conducted solely by the supervisor	Conducted with the supervisee

focusing on the areas they have focused on and, perhaps, on helping them identify possible affect-oriented opportunities for future sessions.

A fourth difference between behaviorist and constructivist assessment is that behaviorist assessments are typically conducted solely by the supervisor, using criteria developed or selected by the supervisor. Assessment, from a constructivist perspective however, is often framed as a "self-referent construction" (Guidano, 1995, p. 101), which necessitates the co-construction of assessment criteria and outcomes. Constructivists, thus, typically conduct assessment *with* supervisees and often involve supervisees in the selection of goals and measures to assess these goals. This does not mean that constructive supervisors abandon the responsibility of assessment; rather, they seek to share this responsibility with supervisees. The goal of constructivist assessment, therefore, is not just to provide the supervisor's view of the supervisee, but to encourage supervisees to engage in their own process of self-evaluation.

This comparison between constructivist and behaviorist views about assessment highlights some of the distinguishing features of constructivists assessment, which range from viewing assessment as a part of an intervention, to co-constructing assessment criteria with supervisees. These fundamental concepts regarding constructivist assessment provide important implications for how constructive supervisors conduct assessment procedures. In the next section, I provide an overview of how these constructivist ideas about assessment are integrated into the constructive approach to supervision.

Beginning the Assessment Process

Consistent with all forms of assessment, the process of assessment in constructive supervision begins at the very first supervision meeting. However, unlike many traditional forms of supervision, where supervisors delineate expectations for supervisees, constructive supervisors begin by asking supervisees to describe their expectations for supervision and their preferred learning objectives and goals. This process of establishing mutual goals, which is highly consistent with constructivist ideas of assessment, is also positively correlated with strong supervisor/supervisee working alliance and supervisee satisfaction with supervision (Lehrman-Waterman & Ladanay, 2001). Additionally, supervisors can ask supervisees to share information about their prior experiences in supervision and to describe elements of these experiences that they perceived as helpful or unhelpful to their counseling development. These supervisee-directed goals, along with their descriptions of their prior supervision experiences, can stimulate conversations about what supervisees would like to receive from supervisors to help them attain these goals.

Once supervisee goals for supervision have been articulated and discussed, supervisors can then begin to frame assessment procedures by providing supervisees with an overview of the process of constructive supervision. Briefly outlining the basic premises of constructive supervision is important, as it can be significantly different from what supervisees may expect when entering a supervisory relationship. The following is one example of how the principles of constructive supervision can be articulated to supervisees in this initial meeting and/or in a written disclosure statement:

> My orientation to clinical supervision is based upon the Constructive Approach, which recognizes that supervisees have within them the ability to guide their own learning during supervision. Instead of providing you with a lot of direct advice or instruction, our sessions will focus largely on allowing you the opportunity to critically, yet non-judgmentally, reflect on your experiences so that you develop more sophisticated understandings of your clients, yourself, and your role as a helper. This process requires that you do a great deal of reflecting on what occurred in your counseling sessions, as well as your thoughts and emotions as we process these experiences together. The process also necessitates an open and creative exploration about how your personal issues may be affecting the ways in which you approach therapy and supervision. My role will be to help you critically assess all of your experiences so that you can identify what you know; how you came to these ideas; and, most importantly, the strengths and limitations of your ideas. I will do this by asking a lot of reflective questions and introducing several reflective-based activities, which you will complete during and outside of our supervision sessions. While I am excited to see and learn about your successes with clients, I am also interested in having you share experiences that were confusing, frustrating, or unproductive, as I believe that reflecting on these experiences provides the most fruitful opportunities for growth. Due to this emphasis on self-reflection, the assessment process will involve not only assessing your counseling skills and abilities, but also your ability to critically and openly self-reflect upon these experiences in meaningful ways and to develop new knowledge based on these reflections.

After briefly outlining the process of constructive supervision, supervisors can then discuss fundamental logistical aspects of supervision such as meeting times (including cancellation procedures), paperwork that must be submitted, limits of confidentiality, and the sources from which supervisors will draw their evaluations. Sources of evaluation can include tapes of supervisees working with clients, their reflections about their interactions with clients, and other supporting documents such as reflective essays or assessments from clients. While supervisors will be able to glean a great deal about their supervisee's counseling skills through watching their counseling sessions, supervisors need to be cautious not to rely too heavily on tape performance to rate supervisees or they risk having supervisees present only segments which they believe were successful (as opposed to presenting segments for which they want help). Constructive supervisors can facilitate this process by gently reminding supervisees that they will be assessed as much on how they think about and reflect upon their tapes as they are on the actual tape performance.

After the process of constructive supervision has been thoroughly discussed and supervisees are informed about the logistical aspects of the supervision experience, the specific procedures for conducting assessment need to be identified and discussed. This includes identifying the assessment activities and formal assessment instruments that supervisors will use to conduct their assessments, which is described below.

Constructive Assessment Activities and Instruments

Constructive supervisors often integrate a wide range of assessment activities and instruments. The core of constructive assessment, however, revolves around supervisee self-assessment. In this section I begin by suggesting strategies for facilitating supervisee self-assessment from a constructive approach. Next I describe how to integrate more formal, standardized forms of assessment into the practice of constructive supervision. I conclude this section by describing an assessment instrument that can be used by constructive supervisors to formally assess supervisee development from a constructive perspective.

Supervisee Self-Assessment

As outlined earlier, a core objective of constructive assessment, and perhaps the aspect that distinguishes it most from other approaches to assessment, is the emphasis on supervisee self-assessment. Encouraging supervisee self-assessment has been found to be positively correlated with higher levels of critical self-reflection (Kadushin, 1992) and can empower supervisees to engage in self-assessment throughout their professional careers (Haynes, Corey, & Moulton, 2003). Yet self-assessment can also be one of the most difficult aspects of supervision. A common concern about supervisee self-assessment is that newer counselors or counselors-in-training are unable to accurately self-assess because they lack experience or an understanding of the field. Research on the efficacy of self-assessment, however, has been mixed (Bernard & Goodyear, 2014). While some studies have demonstrated that supervisees, including new graduate students, can provide accurate assessment (e.g., Dowling, 1984), other scholars have suggested the task is too complex for supervisees to effectively conduct on their own (e.g., Barnes, 2004).

This conflicting research suggests the need for supervisors to carefully position supervisee self-assessment procedures in ways that allow them to succeed in this complex task. Fortunately, the core ingredients of the constructive approach are designed to enhance critical self-reflection, which can facilitate self-assessment skills. While not all supervisees will initially be comfortable conducting self-assessments, this process will eventually become easier for them as the process of constructive supervision evolves and supervisee self-reflection becomes the primary focus of the intervention. However, constructive supervisors can also integrate several activities designed to promote self-assessment skills from a constructivist framework. The following three activities were adapted from activities used by constructivist psychotherapists to facilitate self-assessment in clients. After providing details on how supervisors can conduct these three self-assessment activities, I will conclude the section by providing general guidelines for facilitating skills of self-assessment in small group supervision.

Self-Characterization Sketch

The first activity, called the *Self-Characterization Sketch*, is an assessment procedure originally developed by George Kelly, who is widely regarded as the founder of the constructivist psychotherapy movement. This activity synthesizes aspects of general semantics (Korzybski, 1933) and psychodrama (Moreno, 1937) to help clients understand the ways in which they organize and structure their understandings of the world and how their current behaviors are impacted by these self-organizing structures. The activity is also designed to provide a "springboard for experimentation with alternative self-constructions" (Neimeyer, 1993, p. 83) that can lead to new behaviors that are more adaptive to their evolving constructions of the world. Below, I will describe how the activity can be adapted to facilitate self-assessment in supervisees.

To begin, supervisors ask supervisees to write a self-characterization of themselves as counselors, but to write in the third person as if they were describing a character in a play. Writing in the third person, according to Kelly, is crucial as it helps minimize resistance that can be associated with formal self-analyses. Writing in the third person also encourages a more free-flowing, holistic perspective on their emerging identity. Supervisees should be encouraged to begin their characterization sketch by addressing areas that might be easier to discuss, like the aspects of counseling they find most enjoyable and their perceived strengths as counselors.

After writing about their character's perceived strengths and areas they enjoy, the characterization then moves to addressing more difficult aspects, including describing client issues with which they are uncomfortable and identifying areas of counseling in which they are struggling. Supervisees are encouraged to provide detailed examples of their character's limitations in these areas and to be specific in describing the thoughts and feelings associated with their examples. This aspect of the characterization sketch should also include exploring the possible origins of their beliefs surrounding these issues, the implications of their struggles to their work with clients and their own growth and development as counselors, and steps they might take to overcome these limitations.

To assist supervisors in utilizing supervisee self-characterization sketches, Neimeyer (1993) provided a list of guidelines for analyzing the self-characterization sketch. Although Neimeyer's guidelines were written for psychotherapists who were reviewing clients' self-characterization sketches, several of the guidelines are useful for supervisors to consider when using the activity with supervisees. First, he recommends that readers take a credulous approach in which the writer's views are not doubted. Rather than critiquing the views or seeking to obtain hidden or underlying issues, the supervisor's main goal is to simply try to understand supervisees' views of counseling and their relationship to the field at that moment. He also recommended that readers examine the sketch holistically, reflecting on each statement against the context of the entire sketch. This can include looking for themes that are repeated (including emotions such as anger or fear), the roles that are implied in each statement, and the evidence that supervisees use to substantiate their perspectives. Finally, Neimeyer urges readers to consider this as a developmental activity, rather than as a stand-alone assessment, and to assume writers are working at the "growing edge" of self-understanding (p. 85). This last statement is perhaps the most important as it denotes the recursive nature of the activity in bridging both assessment and intervention; as supervisees begin self-assessing current understandings of themselves in relation to the field, the process is also initiating new ideas, understandings, and additional questions for them to consider. This activity, therefore, provides a potentially meaningful tool for encouraging supervisees to creatively self-assess their abilities and to develop future goals and learning objectives.

Sine-Wave Activity

A second activity that was originally designed for use in constructivist psychotherapy, but that also has utility in facilitating self-assessment skills in supervisees, is the *Sine-Wave Activity* (Steenbarger & Pels, 1997). In this activity, supervisors ask supervisees to represent their experiences with clients by drawing a wave, with peeks of the wave being times they felt especially competent or effective, and valleys being times they felt ineffective. The activity can be conducted in several different ways to meet a wide range of assessment needs. One way is to provide open-ended directions that allow supervisees to explore the areas that are most meaningful to them at that time. Supervisors can also frame the activity in a more specific way by asking supervisees to critique a particular session using several different criteria that were established earlier, such as listening skills, case conceptualization skills, multicultural awareness and skills, or intervention procedures. Similarly, the activity can be used as a tool for supervisees to assess their progress throughout the supervision experience by allowing them to chart their experiences over a course of days, weeks, or months.

Archeology of Supervision Activity

A third constructivist psychotherapy activity that can be adapted to facilitate supervisee self-assessment is the *Archeology of Therapy Activity* (Epston & White, 1995). Unlike the previous two assessment activities, which can be utilized at any point during the supervision experience, this activity is designed specifically for the final supervision session. Epston and White developed the activity in reaction to the frequent positioning of termination in therapy as loss for clients, which they believed reinforced dependency on the counselor while marginalizing the accomplishments and independence of the client. Rather than positioning the end of counseling as loss, this activity positions it as an important right of passage and allows clients the opportunity to formally celebrate growth and accomplishments, while also acknowledging areas in need of continued work. Inherent in this process of self-assessment is that clients consider themselves "consultants to themselves" (p. 345), thus insisting they establish personal agency regarding their own growth and learning.

For counselors-in-training, the activity can be used to help mark supervisees' educational transitions, such as those that occur when students move from practicum to internship, or during their final supervision experience before graduating and becoming professional counselors. It can also be used with professional counselors to mark various professional milestones that can include promotions, career changes, or transitions from one supervisor to another.

Supervisors wishing to implement this activity will inform supervisees early on that their final supervision session is devoted to providing them the opportunity to document their learning that has occurred throughout the course of supervision. This learning can involve things they have learned about themselves, their understandings about counseling theories and techniques, their abilities to work with particular clients or client issues, or any other meaningful learning experiences. In preparation for this final meeting, supervisees are instructed not only to present their learning in these areas, but also to provide evidence of that learning, which can include videotaped segments, case notes, transcripts, or personal journals.

To help facilitate this reflective process, supervisors can provide supervisees with sample questions to help orient them toward the task. The questions are designed to encourage a "grammar of agency," allowing supervisees to play an active role in constructing the meaning of the experience rather than just attributing their success purely to the work of the supervisor (Epston & White, 1995, p. 346). Epston and White provided five different types of questions to give to clients who are preparing for this psychotherapy capstone session; of these five groups of questions, the first two (orientation and unique account questions) lend themselves best to facilitating supervisee self-assessment at the conclusion of clinical supervision. The following are some examples of orientation questions, adapted from Epson and White's list, which can be used when implementing the activity in clinical supervision:

- Which of the strategies that you have developed can be most useful to you in the future? How can you remember to use this strategy?
- What personal qualities were most helpful in allowing you to achieve this strategy?
- What advice would you give yourself in the future for handling problems that might arise?
- What advice might you give other counselors who are struggling with the same issues that you struggled with during supervision?
- How might you, as a future supervisor, help a supervisee who is experiencing similar developmental challenges as a therapist?

Next, supervisors can move from asking general orienting questions to more specific "account questions" that help supervisees specify their solutions should they face similar situations in the future (Epston & White, 1995, p. 348). Examples of these questions include the following:

- Can you give me a specific, step-by-step guide on how you arrived at this new understanding?
- What did you notice about yourself that led to this realization? What other characteristics about you helped you develop this new understanding?
- What aspects of your history provided you with the foundation to develop this new understanding?

These reflective questions allow supervisees not only to resurrect meaningful learning experiences, but also to carefully reflect upon these experiences by delineating the conditions under which this learning occurred. This is a process that encourages supervisees to move from being passive recipients of knowledge to becoming "knowledge makers" (p. 352), thus decreasing dependency on their supervisors and increasing reliance on themselves.

While any of the three activities mentioned previously in this section can be conducted in small groups, the process of self-assessment can also be facilitated in small groups without the use of structured activities. Inevitably, supervisees who present their tapes in small groups will compare their own work to those of their peers who are presenting their own counseling tapes in the group. In my experience, supervisees who are struggling in their counseling sessions will notice (and often comment upon) the successful work of their peers. In some cases, the struggling supervisee will actually seek advice or suggestions from peers who appear to them to be more proficient, or even attempt to emulate some of the things these peers have done. Unlike gaining advice that is handed down from an all-knowing supervisor, advice gained from peers does not, in my experience, lead to supervisees becoming dependent upon each other for answers. This is likely due to the fact that peer supervisees have a more egalitarian relationship to each other than to the supervisor. As a result, the process often leads to a more collaborative exploration of how to help each other improve.

This process is facilitated when supervisors teach group members the fundamental principles of the constructive approach and model for them how to respond to each other in ways that facilitate critical self-reflection. Small group supervision, therefore, when properly facilitated, can actually assist in the process of self-assessment by providing supervisees with exemplars from which to compare and contrast their own work, along with peers with whom they can consult.

The activities described above provide opportunities for supervisors to facilitate supervisee self-assessment skills by encouraging them to become experts on their own experiences and the learning that resulted from these experiences. Yet self-assessment activities are only one aspect of constructive assessment. Constructive supervisors also integrate formal assessment procedures into their assessment processes. In the next section, I will describe the ways in which formal assessments can be used to assess supervisees from a constructive perspective.

Integrating Formal Assessment Instruments

In his review of constructivist assessment in psychotherapy, Neimeyer (1993) repeatedly emphasized that constructivist assessment is not intended to supplant other, more formal means of assessment. Rather, Neimeyer argued, constructivist assessment can be integrated to enhance the assessment process by capturing the idiographic and phenomenological nature of clients' experiences. Similarly, constructive supervisors also integrate formal assessment instruments in order to assess dimensions of counseling that are relevant to the various settings in which supervisees conduct their counseling. Such assessments may focus on basic skills for supervisees who are new trainees, to more advanced assessments that focus on particular elements of counseling for senior practitioners.[1]

Use of standardized assessment instruments does not, however, automatically equate to ignoring the process of supervisee self-assessment. In fact, a common procedure used by supervisors from various supervision traditions is to ask supervisees to complete their own self-assessments using the particular instrument the supervisor, agency, or training institution has selected. The results of this self-assessment can then be shared with supervisors to facilitate conversations about supervisee progress in the areas identified in the instrument and to mutually address areas in need of improvement.

In addition to allowing supervisees to provide self-assessments using formalized assessment instruments, constructive supervisors can also complete their own evaluations of supervisees using these instruments. When doing so, supervisors need to clearly explain their rating criteria. While all assessment instruments provide definitions of each rating criteria, these descriptions are often worded broadly and in ways that allow for varying interpretations of what each rating point should look like. Supervisors also have different views about the general notion of rating that can affect the ways in which they rate supervisees, irrespective of how clearly the rating criteria are delineated in the instruments. Some supervisors may, for example, refuse to give high scores to supervisees in their earlier sessions, even if they are doing excellent work, because they believe the lower score will provide supervisees with more motivation to continue to develop and grow. Neufeldt (2007), for example, recommends that practicum student supervisees should not expect ratings above a 2 or 3 (on a 5 point scale) for this reason.

While I strongly agree with much of Neufeldt's (2007) reflective approach to supervision, I disagree that supervisees will automatically interpret high ratings from supervisors as signals that additional learning and growth is not needed. On the contrary, I often provide supervisees with high ratings, even new trainees, if they demonstrate skills that are exemplary for someone at that stage of their development. From my experience, high ratings, when warranted, can facilitate intrinsic motivation to achieve mastery in order to more effectively help their clients (as opposed to improving only to gain a good rating from the supervisor[2]). While inter-rater reliability is likely to vary greatly on any assessment instrument used in clinical supervision, the important point is that supervisors clearly explain their rating systems in the beginning of the supervision experience. If a supervisor considers a "5" unattainable for newer trainees, it needs to be clearly explained to supervisees, along with the rationale for this lowered rating system. Likewise, supervisors who provide higher ratings to supervisees of any developmental level should explain that the "5" simply means that they are doing great for someone at their level, while stressing that there is always room to improve.

While constructive supervisors can integrate a wide range of assessment instruments into the process of supervisee assessment, the process in which they use the instruments needs to remain closely tied to the constructivist principles of learning and development upon which the approach is based. This includes establishing a close, egalitarian relationship; empowering supervisees to actively participate in their own assessment; conveying feedback in a way that is clear, but empathic; using descriptive rather than judgmental language; and, perhaps most importantly, helping supervisees contextualize the feedback as opportunities for growth rather than criticism.

The dimensions that will be assessed by the instrument also need to be discussed regularly throughout the supervision experience. While it is not necessary for supervisors to provide a formal, written assessment at the conclusion of each supervision session, they should provide supervisees with regular, ongoing feedback (often referred to as "formative feedback") regarding their assessments of supervisees on the dimensions outlined in the instruments they are using. This allows supervisees the opportunity to address supervisor concerns before receiving a final evaluation and to receive regular feedback on their progress. Supervisees should never be blindsided with a negative evaluation at the conclusion of supervision.

In addition to integrating standard assessment instruments, I have also developed an instrument for assessing supervisee growth and development specifically from a constructive perspective. Rather than focusing on assessing particular counseling skills, as is the case with most other clinical supervision assessment instruments, the questions in the *Constructive Supervision Assessment* (CSA) focus on assessing various dimensions of supervisee critical self-reflection, which includes areas such as creativity; risk-taking; thinking openly and deeply about critical issues; being patient with themselves; and using descriptive, non-judgmental language. The scale also assesses supervisee abilities to use their own experiences and personal constructs in understanding client issues, along with consulting with colleagues and professional literature, while also critically evaluating all of the sources from which they draw their hypotheses. Additionally, the scale assesses the extent to which they have openly explored how their own biases and defenses have affected their views of clients and their work in supervision. The instrument, which has not yet undergone any testing of validity or reliability, is available in the back of this book (see Appendix).

Providing Difficult Feedback to Supervisees

While the constructive approach is often successful in allowing supervisees to proactively identify areas in which they need to improve and develop their own plans for improvement, the process does not guarantee that all supervisees will attain proficiency in all required areas, or that they will effectively identify all areas in need of improvement. In my experience, some supervisees who may struggle in the counseling role can resist engaging in meaningful self-assessment by continually focusing their reflections on more superficial aspects of counseling rather than reflecting on deeper areas in which they are struggling. Other supervisees may simply fail to recognize any limitations in their work or to reflect in meaningful ways on these limitations. In these instances, constructive supervisors can integrate a more directive approach for communicating this difficult feedback to supervisees.

From my experience, the less comfortable supervisors are in giving constructive feedback, the worse they are at it. Supervisors who are the most uncomfortable giving constructive feedback tend to either ignore it until it is too late, or present it in ways that are too soft for supervisees to fully grasp their deficit areas. Ironically, I have also noted times when supervisors who disclose strong discomfort in the area of evaluation can also present feedback to supervisees in ways that are overly harsh or critical. Supervisors, therefore, must become comfortable themselves with this process in order to effectively provide support to their supervisees.

When instances arise where supervisors must provide critical feedback to supervisees, it can be useful to follow the suggestions provided by Bernard and Goodyear (2014), which include (a) balancing critical feedback with feedback that is supportive, (b) clearly delineating areas in need of improvement by providing examples based on specific behaviors, and (c) connecting the critique to the learning outcomes that were established at the beginning of the supervision process. I have also found that the principles of mindfulness can be extremely helpful for both supervisees and supervisors when discussing areas in need of improvement. This includes not only engaging in mindfulness-based activities (see Chapter 4), but also presenting feedback in ways that are descriptive rather than using judgmental language such as "good" or "bad." Most importantly is the ability of the supervisor to position the limitations as an opportunity for supervisee growth by encouraging supervisees to develop their own action plans for addressing the limitations. Additionally, to help reinforce the collaborative nature of the relationship, supervisors can also position this discussion as an opportunity to solicit feedback from supervisees about their work as supervisors. Specifically, supervisors can ask supervisees how they can help them attain the competencies that supervisors have identified as needing improvement.

The following example illustrates one way in which a supervisor can begin to sensitively, yet clearly express concern about a supervisee's progress in attaining a particular competency from a constructive approach. In this case, the issue revolves around a supervisee's inability to formulate a meaningful case conceptualization, which is common issue among counselors-in-training.

SUPERVISOR: For the past three sessions, I have asked you to try formulating some hypotheses about what is going on with your client and you have struggled to develop ideas about her.

SUPERVISEE: Yes, it's been difficult for me to understand just what is going on with her. I know it's not the way you operate, but I sometimes wish that you would just help me and give me your thoughts about what's going on with her.

SUPERVISOR: As you know, case conceptualization is a central task of counseling. I could certainly provide you with my own ideas about your client, but my sense is that I can help you become a better counselor by helping you learn to develop your own ideas. I also believe that you are the expert on her problems since she is your client; you are the one who works with her every week and you know her better than nearly anyone else.

SUPERVISEE: I suppose you are right in that regard. I do know her quite well by now. I'm not sure why it's so difficult for me to conceptualize her problems.

SUPERVISOR: Until you can develop a conceptualization of what is going on with your client, it is going to be difficult for you to move forward with her. Additionally, I need to be able to document that you have

developed case conceptualization skills in order for you to successfully complete this experience. I'm really interested in seeing you
succeed, and I know you have within you the ability to develop
your own conceptualizations of this client's issues. Perhaps we can
spend some time now discussing ways in which I can better assist
you in finding these answers?

In this example, the supervisor is addressing the importance of the supervisee
developing case conceptualization skills, not only to be able to assist the client,
but also to successfully complete the supervision experience. At the same time
that the supervisor is clearly expressing the need for progress, she is also expressing faith in the supervisee's abilities to discover her own answers and indicating a
willingness to try new things in order to effectively help the supervisee succeed.
As all experienced supervisors know, however, even critiques that are presented in
the most sensitive, constructive, and mindful ways can initiate painful emotional
reactions in supervisees. It is, therefore, important to also briefly touch on the
issue of dealing with supervisee strong emotional reactions, including anger and
tears, in the context of supervisee assessment.

The first time I had a supervisee burst into tears while discussing her assessment was when I was a doctoral student participating in one of my early experiences as a supervisor. I was conducting the supervision as a requirement for my
doctoral-level supervision class and, as a result, the session was taped. Feeling
uncomfortable with what had transpired, I decided to present the session to my
class to illicit feedback on what I had done wrong. To my surprise, some of my
peers, upon watching the session, quickly focused their critiques on the supervisee
rather than on me. Their assessments ranged from her trying to manipulate me
by playing a victim, to diagnosing her as having a series of personality disorders.

While I was somewhat relieved that my peers were not focusing their critiques on my behavior, I was also concerned that they were being too harsh on
the supervisee. I had worked with this supervisee for several weeks at this point
and she did not strike me as manipulative or as having any sort of serious diag-
noses. I simply viewed her as upset to learn that I felt she was struggling. Perhaps
it would be more accurate to state that she was upset to hear that I knew she
was struggling, since she later admitted that she also had felt uncomfortable and
incompetent in the areas I had critiqued. Rather than vigorously defending my
actions to my instructor and fellow students, as I had anticipated, I ended up
defending the supervisee by outlining areas in which she had succeeded and normalizing her emotional reaction.

Since that early supervision session, I have had dozens of other supervisees
burst into tears during supervision and I have actually come to understand it as
a somewhat normal process for many supervisees. This is not to imply that tears
must occur for supervisees to grow in meaningful ways (most of my supervisees have not cried), but it can be a growth-promoting experience when openly
addressed and embraced by both the supervisor and the supervisee. I also believe

that the constructive approach, with its emphasis on exploring deep emotion within the context of an empathic supervisor/supervisee relationship, can lend itself more to intense emotional reactions than other supervision approaches. As a result, it is important for constructive supervisors to be comfortable with and prepared for working with strong supervisee emotions during the course of constructive clinical supervision.

When tears arise, it has been my practice to begin by empathically acknowledging the emotion, like I would if I were counseling a client (e.g., I can see this is really hard for you). Often this type of reflection leads to supervisees exploring more deeply the emotional content behind the tears, which can be related to things like wanting to do well, be more effective in helping their clients, or even feeling as if they have somehow let down their supervisor. Supervisees will also often discuss their fears of not doing well and their frustrations in working so hard without getting the sense of satisfaction or success that they believe is warranted by their degree of effort. At some point afterward, they often state how embarrassed they are to have broken down in front of me. This state of "being upset about being upset" can cause some supervisees to rigidify and shut down, so I have found it important to normalize their experiences. In my case, I am able to tell them with confidence that I have had many other supervisees shed tears in my office and that I consider it an important part of the process of becoming a counselor. If fact, I explain that these types of *breakdowns* can often lead to *breakthroughs*, in terms of both outcomes with clients and their own relationships to the field. I also seek to normalize whatever the difficulty is that they are experiencing as counselors and express my confidence in their abilities to overcome this obstacle.

Perhaps most importantly, I tell supervisees that I believe they can succeed and that I will keep working with them as long as it takes for them to master whatever difficulties they have encountered. This is easy for me to say because it is something that I genuinely believe to be true. All supervisees, in my opinion, can succeed in the field, despite whatever challenges or dysfunctional behavior is manifesting at the time. The key, I instruct them, is to have faith in themselves and the process of supervision, and to continue to work hard. The "hard work" can take many different forms, from engaging in additional reading, counseling experiences, or reflective activities, to seeing their own counselor to assist them in recognizing and overcoming issues that may be preventing them from fully engaging in the therapeutic process with their clients. In my context as a counselor educator, this can mean extending their supervised counseling experiences beyond the semester schedule, or even requiring that they redo the experiences again the next semester.

While supervisees are seldom happy to learn that they have additional tasks before successfully completing their supervision experiences, many do seem somewhat relieved to gain extra time and experience. As I stated earlier, most supervisees who are struggling know that they are struggling; while the initial recognition of this from their supervisor may spur an emotional reaction, ultimately, it has been my experience that supervisees will come to understand their need to continue to work to improve in order to work effectively with clients. This is not to imply that all supervisees will choose to engage in the extra work or attain the desired competencies upon completion of this work. However, I believe that a supervisor who demonstrates a belief in supervisees' abilities to improve and a commitment to help them attain success is often more valued by supervisees than those who push supervisees along without addressing their deficit areas.

Chapter Summary

In this chapter I have provided a description of supervisee assessment procedures from a constructive perspective. This included delineating key differences between constructivist principles of assessment and those used in traditional, behaviorist approaches to assessment. I also provided a description of how constructivist principles of assessment can be integrated into clinical supervision assessment, which included activities for encouraging supervisee self-assessment, integrating constructive principles of assessment with traditional forms of assessment, and an instrument that can be used to assess supervisee growth and development specifically from a constructive perspective. I concluded this chapter by providing suggestions on how to present difficult feedback to supervisees who require additional learning experiences to attain required competencies. In the next chapter, I provide answers to some common questions about the constructive approach, including additional questions readers may have about conducting supervisee assessment.

Notes

1 For a detailed review and critique of potential assessment instruments, readers are referred to Ellis, D'Iuso, and Ladany (2008).
2 Readers should refer to the Self-Determination Theory section in Chapter 2 for a more detailed review of intrinsic and extrinsic motivation.

References

Barnes, K.L. (2004). Applying self-efficacy theory to counselor training and supervision: A comparison of two approaches. *Counselor Education and Supervision, 44*(1), 56–69.

Bernard, J.M., & Goodyear, R.K. (2014). *Fundamentals of clinical supervision*. Boston: Merrill.

Dowling, S. (1984). Clinical evaluation: A comparison of self, self with videotape, peers, and supervisors. *The Clinical Supervisor, 2*(3), 71–78.

Ellis, M.V., D'Iuso, N., & Ladany, N. (2008). State of the art in the assessment, measurement, and evaluation of clinical supervision. In A.K. Hess, K.D. Hess & T.H. Hess (Eds.), *Psychotherapy supervision: Theory, research, and practice* (2nd ed., pp. 473–499). New York: John Wiley.

Epston, D., & White, M. (1995). Termination as a rite of passage: Questioning strategies for a therapy of inclusion. In R.A. Neimeyer, & M.J. Mahoney (Eds.), *Constructivisim in psychotherapy* (pp. 339–356). Washington, DC: American Psychological Association.

Guidano, V.F. (1995). Constructivist psychotherapy: A theoretical framework. In R.A. Nei-meyer, & M.J. Mahoney (Eds.), *Constructivism in psychotherapy* (pp. 93–110). Washington, DC: American Psychological Association.

Haynes, R., Corey, G., & Moulton, P. (2003). *Clinical supervision in the helping professions: A practical guide* (1st ed.). Pacific Grove, CA: Brooks Cole.

Hoffman, M.A., Hill, C.E., Holmes, S.E., & Freitas, G.F. (2005). Supervisor perspective on the process and outcome of giving easy, difficult, or no feedback to supervisees. *Journal of Counseling Psychology, 52*(1), 3–13.

Kadushin, A. (1992). *Supervision in social work.* New York: Columbia University Press.

Korzybski, A. (1933; 2d ed., 1941; 3d ed., 1948). *Science and sanity: An introduction to non-Aristotelian systems and general semantics.* Lakeville, CN: International Non-Aristotelian Library Publishing Co.

Ladany, N., Lehrman-Waterman, D., Molinaro, M., & Wolgast, B. (1999). Psychotherapy supervisor ethical practices adherence to guidelines, the supervisory working alliance, and supervisee satisfaction. *The Counseling Psychologist, 27*(3), 443–475.

Lehrman-Waterman, D., & Ladany, N. (2001). Development and validation of the evalua-tion process within supervision inventory [special issue]. *Journal of Counseling Psychology, 48*(2), 168–177.

Moreno, J.L. (1937). Inter-personal therapy and the psychopathology of inter-personal relations. *Sociometry, 1*(1–2), 9–76.

Neimeyer, G.J. (1993). *Constructivist assessment: A casebook.* Counseling psychologist case-book series, vol. 2. Thousand Oaks, CA: Sage.

Neufeldt, S.A. (2007). *Supervision strategies for the first practicum* (3rd ed.). Washington, DC: American Counseling Association.

Steenbarger, B.N., & Pels, L.C. (1997). Constructivist foundations for multicultural coun-seling: Assessment and intervention. In T.L. Sexton & B.L. Griffen (Eds.), *Constructiv-ist thinking in counseling practice, research, and training* (pp. 111–121). New York: Teachers College Press.

6

ANSWERS TO COMMON QUESTIONS ABOUT CONSTRUCTIVE CLINICAL SUPERVISION

In this final chapter, I provide answers to a number of questions about the theory that have been asked by students during clinical supervision classes, colleagues during professional presentations and discussions, and reviewers and editors of this book. Topics range from how to ethically manage gatekeeping responsibilities, how to work with supervisees who struggle in developing their own answers, and the experiences that led me to consider supervision in this way. These questions have been invaluable in assisting me in thinking more deeply about the approach; it is my hope that my answers to them will provide readers with additional clarity regarding the more applied aspects of the approach and the rationale behind these applications. I have listed each question below in bold, and placed my answer to each one directly underneath the question, in an effort to replicate an actual encounter with a person answering a question.

How can you assert (in Chapter 1) that the main purpose of supervision, from a constructive perspective, is to facilitate supervisee development when the focus should always be to protect clients? Aren't we causing harm to clients and society if we focus largely on supervisee development at the expense of monitoring and gatekeeping?

This question regarding supervisor roles and responsibilities is central in understanding a fundamental element of the constructive approach, and more broadly, the role of constructivism in the helping professions. Indeed, while most definitions of supervision recognize the need to both protect clients *and* facilitate supervisee development, supervision researchers and practitioners have often prioritized the gatekeeping function above that of facilitating supervisee development (Speedy, 2010). As the question above indicates, some supervisors believe the ethical mandate to protect client welfare should always trump a focus of supervisee development.

Interestingly, there is no research to support the long-held belief that supervision focused on gatekeeping and monitoring provides any more protection to clients than supervision that is focused on supervisee development. Wheeler and Richards (2007) and Watkins (2011) both conducted in-depth reviews of supervision research and concluded that while supervision has been proven to enhance supervisee development in a number of areas, including self-awareness, intervention knowledge, counseling skills, and self-efficacy, neither review found any research to support the assertion that supervision contributed in any way to client outcomes, including protecting clients from harmful counseling.

Other research has indicated just how complex the roles of monitoring and gatekeeping are for supervisors. King and Wheeler (2007) conducted a qualitative study of ten experts in the field of counseling and supervision in Britain (where supervision is required for all practicing therapists) to understand their perspectives of supervision, including their views of monitoring and gatekeeping. All the participants supervised counselors in private practice settings rather than professional training programs. The results indicated that even among expert supervisors, there was a lack of clarity regarding their roles as gatekeepers and protectors of clients. The researchers concluded, "The notion that all casework is monitored by an experienced and qualified colleague is a fantasy, not a reality. Most counseling work is not discussed in supervision, and the notion of the supervisor 'overseeing' the work of the counselor is naïve. The expectations that the profession currently has of the supervisory process are unrealistic" (p. 227). Yet despite a lack of empirical evidence supporting the efficacy of the monitoring role in protecting client welfare, and research suggesting that it is unrealistic for supervisors to assume this function in a meaningful way, many in the field continue to view the role of the supervisor primarily as a monitor and gatekeeper.

So, if monitoring client welfare is impossible, and if there is no research that it actually helps protect clients or improve therapeutic outcomes, why is this notion of protection so ingrained into our understanding of clinical supervision?

The idea regarding the need to monitor all supervisee activities in order to protect clients is rooted in a positivist worldview where supervisors are expected to be all-knowing and supervisee knowledge and experience are devalued. This positivist prioritizing of professional knowledge over more localized and experience-based knowledge has been challenged by a number of supervisors, most notably, by those who adhere to a narrative approach. Narrative supervisors, such as Speedy (2010), view the positivist positioning of knowledge as merely one possibility, or "story" that has emerged within the profession among many possible alternatives to understanding the role and function of supervision, even in the area of professional ethics. As Speedy (2010) has stated, "In abandoning the authoritative truth of a particular story of how human beings work, narrative practitioners have abandoned the authority of traditional normative ethics in [favor] of ethical pluralism and a valuing of diversity of ethical stances that may come with different stories and positions" (p. 426). This narrative tradition of "ethical pluralism" is not one that ignores professional ethics and gatekeeping responsibilities, but rather expands the ethical arena of supervision to include multiple forms of knowledge that arise from experience.

Are you saying then that there are no rights or wrongs in counseling ethics?

No, constructive supervisors recognize that supervisees can make ethical mistakes that require direct supervisor intervention to protect clients. Examples of clear-cut ethical violations include engaging in romantic relationships with clients, failing to act in instances of homicidal/suicidal ideation, or disclosing confidential material, to name a few. However, the reality is that most ethical issues that arise in supervision are much more complex and do not lend themselves to quick, right-or-wrong assessments from supervisors. Rather, most ethical dilemmas require an in-depth consultation between the supervisee, supervisor, and other professional colleagues in order to fully understand the client population, the norms of the site, and the developmental level of the supervisee.

I am not asserting that supervisors ignore their responsibilities to protect clients and to serve as gatekeepers for the profession when confronted with ethical infractions. However, rather than viewing the supervisor role primarily as one in which they monitor supervisee behaviors looking for mistakes, constructive supervisors encourage supervisees to engage in a process of critical self-reflection that allows them to access and critically reflect upon their own constructions of knowledge regarding ethical dilemmas. From a constructive perspective, ethical missteps provide valuable opportunities for supervisee growth and development.

It is often through the constructive process of normalizing supervisee mistakes and prioritizing reflection of these mistakes that supervisees become comfortable in openly sharing potential ethical dilemmas and mistakes with their supervisors. Additionally, the process of facilitating critical self-reflection regarding ethical concerns, rather than asserting professional knowledge, can often help supervisees develop more nuanced and sophisticated abilities to conceptualize future ethical dilemmas. As Crocket (2004) has noted, some counselors, when reflecting on early supervision experiences, have indicated they felt "little room to grapple with questions . . . when the answers were already being presented, almost before counselors could ask themselves the questions" (p. 180). Crocket argued that when space is given to supervisees to fully explore their own questions and answers, supervisors are provided with a more complete picture of the supervisee's readiness for the field. While research is certainly needed to understand how supervisors can best protect clients and facilitate supervisee ethical decision-making skills, it is possible that the constructive approach can actually minimize client harm when compared to a monitoring-based approach by providing a more welcoming environment for supervisees to disclose potential problems and allowing them meaningful opportunities to learn from the experiences.

I feel it is unethical to allow supervisees to flounder with clients, especially when I have direct experience with the same issues and can offer effective ways for them to deal with their problems. Isn't it better for the client if I teach the supervisee more effective or efficient ways of counseling?

No, not necessarily. Embracing a constructive approach means that supervisors must accept the idea that there are multiple right ways to conduct counseling, and that their "right" way might not be the best approach for this particular counselor with this particular client.

I understand what you are saying, but I can see this approach being very difficult for me since it is very different than the way I was supervised. Do you have any suggestions for helping me become more comfortable accepting that multiple realities and, therefore, multiple "truths" exist in counseling?

I too was taught under a more monitoring-based approach and had difficulty enacting a more reflective approach at first. I understand how difficult it can be to trust and have patience for supervisees to develop their own answers during supervision. One way for supervisors to begin transitioning away from a monitoring-based approach is to examine their own needs to demonstrate competence and expertise to supervisees (see Chapter 1). Additionally, as described earlier, constructive supervisors must accept that their approach, whatever it may be, is not necessarily *better*, or even more expedient than their supervisee's approach. This is an assertion that has been repeatedly demonstrated in research, yet is difficult for many counselors to accept. Speaking to this issue more directly, Speedy (2010) suggested that supervisors regularly clarify their "make-believe" relationship with their supervisee's clients and their tendencies to "makeup heroic stories inside their own heads about the successful outcomes of the clients 'if only they had had me as their counselor'" (p. 423). She goes on to state, "It may be hard to remember, in our enthusiasm to become potent experts in our own right and mentors to our supervisees that our personal, local understandings have as much to offer us as our expert theoretical knowledge" (pp. 426–427). I find Speedy's advice useful whenever I feel I need to become overly assertive with corrections or recommendations for a supervisee.

Shouldn't supervision be about challenging supervisees so they can grow? This constructive approach of accepting their realities seems

to imply that supervisees are always right and, therefore, not forced to grow?

In my experience, having supervised in both a constructive and a traditional, didactic approach, I have found the constructive approach to be more challenging for most of my supervisees. We live in a culture that emphasizes professional knowledge of experts; therefore, many supervisees arrive to supervision assuming a passive role in which knowledge, skills, and evaluation will be transferred to them from their supervisor. The constructive approach can feel much more challenging to them because it encourages supervisees not only to discover their own answers, but also to identify the questions.

What happens when you try all the things you outlined in the book, including the constructive activities, and supervisees still can't develop their own answers? Is it okay then to implement a more didactic approach?

Assuming the conditions outlined in this book have been established, I do not have any problem with supervisors occasionally offering direct advice and suggestions if they can't hold back any longer. But, as I have described throughout the book, supervision focused largely on didactic processes can stifle supervisee creatively and cause dependency on the supervisor for answers. While it has been my experience that most supervisees can rise to the challenge posed by this approach, there are some supervisees who will need extra time to learn the skills of critical self-reflection necessary for professional growth to occur during supervision. As described in Chapter 5, there may be times when additional time and attention is needed.

What if they come up with their own answers, but their answers are not good?

Effective implementation of a constructive approach requires supervisees to continually self-reflect upon all of their thoughts, feeling, and ideas. Often this process of critical self-reflection can occur before supervisees actually implement their ideas. For example, a supervisee who is feeling uneasy about a client who abruptly ended therapy may mention during supervision that he wishes he could have one last conversation with her to gain some closure and clarify why she did not return for therapy. In processing the options for dealing with the ambiguity inherent in this early termination with his client, the supervisee might suggest the possibility of actually contacting the client to ask her why she ended therapy. This option in most (but certainly not all) settings would be an ethical breach. Yet, even this unacceptable conclusion by the supervisee can provide an opportunity for him to critically self-reflect and develop his own answer when approached by the supervisor in constructive manner.

Rather than immediately dismissing the idea, a constructive supervisor could assist the supervisee in exploring this possibility in more detail by asking him what contacting the client would do for him. This question could allow him to explore, in more detail, his feelings about being abandoned by the client or his feeling of inadequacy as a counselor. Next the supervisor could explore how the client might feel about being contacted by the therapist, which would necessarily include exploring both the potential positive things the supervisee might envision his client experiencing from this contact (e.g., wow, he must really care about me!). Finally, the supervisor could ask the supervisee to consult the ethical guidelines of his field and to report his perception of this option, from an ethical standpoint, to the supervisor. In most cases, the supervisee would eventually arrive at a conclusion that this was not a viable option for him. However, by arriving at this decision not to contact the client through this process of critical self-reflection (rather than being told right away not to do it), he is also likely to engage in a process of self-discovery regarding his feeling about his client, himself, and the profession.

Of course, the possibility exists that the supervisor could provide all the right reflective opportunities and the supervisee could still erroneously conclude that it is okay for him to contact the client in the end. In this case, even the most constructive supervisor would need to directly tell the supervisee that it is not okay to contact the client and to educate him about professional ethics and decision making. Yet even if the reflective activity results in the supervisee choosing to make an erroneous decision, this reflective process is still important as it provides a valuable opportunity for supervisee growth. Additionally, it can also provide the supervisor with additional insight about the supervisee's decision-making processes, which would not have been available had the supervisee simply been told "no" at the start.

But isn't it possible that this approach might not be right for all supervisees?

I would agree that some supervisees will have a harder time initially adapting to the subjective, reflective nature of this approach, in much the same way that some clients may initially express resistance to certain approaches to therapy that may not fit with the ways in which they have traditionally conceptualized their problems. Psychotherapy research has demonstrated that clients with a more internalized locus of control tend to fair better in constructivist psychotherapy than those with a more external locus of control (Vincent & LeBow, 1995). Similarly, research has also shown that clients who are more self-reflective, open to new experiences, and who can view their problems as interconnected tend to respond more favorably to constructivist psychotherapeutic approaches than those who are less reflective, closed to new experiences, and who tend to view their problems as a set of disconnected and unrelated individual symptoms (Winter, 1990). However, unlike psychotherapy, where constructivist counselors would seek to refer clients who do not seem amenable to reflective approaches (Neimeyer, 2009), constructive supervisors can effectively work with supervisees who are not initially predisposed to the types of reflective thinking required with constructive supervision.

Rather than referring supervisees who demonstrate a strong external locus of control and a lack of critical self-reflection or abandoning the approach altogether, constructive supervisors can adapt the approach to meet the needs of these supervisees in the same way that a good teacher adapts his approach to meet the diverse learning needs of his students. As described in Chapter 5, this begins by prioritizing the ability to critically self-reflect as a main goal for the supervisee right from the beginning. The process continues by providing the supervisee with regular encouragement to engage in self-reflective processes, both in and out of supervision. Several of the exercises described in Chapter 4 can also be implemented to facilitate supervisee reflexivity.

Throughout this process, supervisors need to be consciously aware of the additional difficulties some supervisee may experiences when being asked to critically self-reflect for the first time, especially those who are from cultures with more modernist educational systems, and to express patience as these supervisees gradually adapt to the new ways of viewing themselves and their clients. Ultimately, it has been my experience that even supervisees who are not predisposed to reflective thinking can learn to become more reflective through judicious use of this approach. In fact, I would assert that it is precisely those supervisees who are not predisposed to the type of reflective thinking inherent in this approach who will benefit the most from it.

Among the numerous theoretical approaches to psychotherapy that are available today, why did you choose these four main theories of psychotherapy (person-centered, SDT, mindfulness, psychoanalytic) to integrate into the constructive approach?

As I described in the introductory chapter, this approach emerged from continuous self-reflection into my own supervision practice. Yet, the lens through which I viewed this practice was undoubtedly shaped by my prior experiences as a counselor and educator, and in dealing with my own problems. While space considerations prevent me from fully detailing the path that has led me to my current understandings of supervision, some readers may find it useful for me to provide a brief overview of how I became aware of and interested in these particular theories that have come to form the backbone of this integrative approach.

As a new counseling professional, I was originally drawn to the cognitive behavioral approach; however, early in my career I began to find the approach incompatible with my growing appreciation for the power of humans to come to their own answers. Rather than battling clients' irrational thinking, I became more interested in helping clients find ways to discover their own meaningful answers. This change regarding my view of human nature led me to consider more humanistic approaches to psychotherapy, which included the person-centered and existential approaches. Not surprisingly, I found these same humanistic ideas were relevant and useful in clinical supervision. The person-centered approach, in particular, with its focus on the relationship and non-directiveness, was particularly useful in providing the framework and tools I needed to allow supervisees to discover their own answers.

At the same time, I also began engaging in a research agenda designed to understand the experiences of college students of color in order to more effectively support and retain them. Through a series of qualitative studies (see Guiffrida & Douthit, 2010 for a review), I learned a great deal about the challenges that many students of color experience at predominately white institutions of higher education. In addition to outlining a number of recommendations for improving the ways in which we prepare and support college students of color, I also became interested in articulating a theory of college student retention that was reflective of the experiences of students of color. In critiquing the leading theory of student retention, offered by Tinto (1993), I discovered that the theory failed to account for student motivation for attending college. In an effort to allow the theory to be more culturally sensitive to the needs of diverse students, I began exploring theories of motivation, and eventually found Self-Determination Theory (SDT) as a useful framework for expanding Tinto's seminal theory (see Guiffrida, 2009; 2006).

Once I became familiar with the principles of SDT, I realized how readily transferrable they were to clinical supervision. Supervisees are often powerfully motivated by intrinsic interests to help their clients and to develop and grow themselves as professionals; the fundamental tenets of SDT (autonomy, competence, and relatedness), therefore, were easily translated into the context of clinical supervision and integrated well with my existing humanistic approach. SDT not only provided me with a framework for understanding how to tap into and support supervisee intrinsic motivation, but it also allowed me to think more deeply about the use of praise, structure, and direct advice in supervision.

I became interested in mindfulness-based approaches based on my personal experience with debilitating back pain. As I became more immersed in the teachings and practice of mindfulness, I began integrating mindfulness into my teaching practices and found it particularly useful in helping students be more present with clients and less apprehensive about evaluation. Based on the success I found in the classroom, I began integrating mindfulness practice into clinical supervision and found similar success with supervisees. Additionally, mindfulness practice also appeared to allow supervisees to be more open and less defensive during supervision, which greatly enhanced their abilities to self-reflect. I was particularly impressed with the ways in which students described mindfulness as assisting them in exploring how personalization issues might be impacting their work with clients. In fact, several supervisees, upon embracing mindful practice, actually seemed excited to explore these issues during supervision and they often described breakthroughs with case conceptualization issues upon taking a non-judgmental inventory of personalization issues. As a result, I began to use the counselor role more often in supervision to help facilitate case conceptualization skills and awareness.

Of course, not all students, even those embracing the self-aware, non-judgmental principles of mindfulness, found it easy to make connections between their own issues and their work with their clients, and some expressed resistance to engaging in this process. Sometimes, supervisees who were extremely open to exploring personalization issues with one client appeared defensive and resistant to engage in this same process when discussing a different client. In an effort to better understand these inconsistent reactions from supervisees to this intervention, I began to study psychodynamic principles of resistance and to explore how unconscious forms of resistance could manifest during supervision. I also began exploring ways of gently, yet persistently addressing supervisee resistance during supervision. These experiments occasionally yielded some powerful supervisee awareness, change, and growth that I do not believe would have been possible without an appreciation for and understanding of the power and influence of unconscious forms of resistance. What was particularly exciting to me is the level of surprise that many supervisees expressed upon realizing these previously unrecognized connections between their internalization issues and their work with their clients. These successful encounters of working with supervisee unconscious resistance led me to integrate this approach regularly during supervision.

As I described in Chapter 2, I have been interested in constructivist pedagogical principles since I first began as a counselor educator. Having realized a number of limitations to the more modernist approach to teaching counseling theories that I was implementing at the time, I began exploring and integrating more constructivist pedagogy into my counselor education classes, which included inquiry-based learning, theories of adult learning, and contemplative practices. Naturally, I began implementing these same principles into my supervision practice and integrating them with the theories of psychotherapy described above. As I garnered more experience in integrating constructivist pedagogical principles with these theories of psychotherapy, I also began teaching these ideas to doctoral students in my clinical supervision courses. I began referring to this approach I was teaching as "constructivist supervision" since the ideas were focused largely on addressing change and growth from a constructivist framework. I realized, however, that the approach I was teaching was quite different from other theories of clinical supervision that used the term "constructivist." My reading list for the course, therefore, consisted of an eclectic and somewhat disjointed mix of readings from philosophy, counselor development, and diverse theories of psychotherapy, which I would then attempt to integrate to students through lectures and discussions.

Despite the limitations of the relatively scattered course reading list, a number of doctoral students began gravitating toward the supervision approach I was teaching, and several of them became very good at it. It was through careful observation of and engagement with their constructivist supervision practice, watching their struggles and successes with the approach, and helping them work through their questions about it, that these ideas began to crystalize for me as a distinct approach. Yet it was not until recently, when several students approached me about studying "constructivist supervision" as their dissertation topic, that I realized the need to formally culminate these ideas in writing since constructivist supervision, as I had taught it, did not yet exist anywhere beyond my classroom.

It was at this point that I sought a way to formally integrate the diverse theories and ideas that I had used to inform my practice of supervision in the form of this book. Thanks to the suggestion of my friend and colleague Andre Marquis, a former student and close friend of Michael Mahoney, I was introduced to Mahoney's developmental–constructivist approach to psychotherapy, which provided the perfect marriage of constructivist ideas of growth, change, and development with theories of psychotherapy. The approach struck me as achieving the rare balance of theoretical depth with practical utility that I was hoping to accomplish with my approach to supervision. Mahoney's constructive theory of psychotherapy, therefore, provided me with the meta-theoretical lens to integrate salient elements of each of these theories of psychotherapy into a practical, theoretically grounded approach to supervision from a constructivist perspective.

These are four distinct theories that would be executed, in counseling practice, very differently. In fact, counselors operating exclusively from any one of these approaches might argue that there are so many epistemological conflicts between them that they would be impossible to integrate together in any meaningful way in therapy. Doesn't this theoretical integration simplify each distinct approach to the point that they are less powerful in practice?

To answer this question, it is important to provide some background on theoretical integration in counseling, since this is a frequent critique of the integrative counseling movement. Theoretical integration arose from the realization that while much research exists regarding the efficacy of psychotherapy when compared to no treatment or placebo groups (Lambert & Begin, 1992), findings from numerous meta-analyses of counseling outcome research have repeatedly failed to acknowledge the consistent superiority of any one particular theory over others (Asay & Lambert, 1999; Wampold, 2001). Many clinicians, in recognizing the inherent inadequacies and strengths of each of the various approaches to psychotherapy, are now seeking ways of integrating salient elements of the various approaches, which has now become a formal movement referred to as theoretical integration (Norcross, 2005).

According to Norcross (2005), the psychotherapy integration movement is "characterized by dissatisfaction with single-school approaches and a concomitant desire to look across school boundaries to see what can be learned from other ways of conducting psychotherapy" (p. 4). There are now hundreds of books in which multiple theories of psychotherapy are synthesized and integrated, and professional associations and journals devoted exclusively to the issue of theoretical integration. Additionally, research suggests that more than half of practicing therapists identify as adhering to multiple theoretical approaches (Jensen, Bergin, & Greaves, 1990; Orlinski et al., 1999). As Rigazio-Digilio, Goncalves, and Ivey (1996) stated, "We have moved from determining which theory is best to discovering how we can integrate and organize what we know" (p. 235).

Many of our existing approaches are actually integrations of what were previously thought to be incompatible approaches to understanding human nature. For example, cognitive behavioral therapy, one of the most popular theories of psychotherapy, integrates two radically different ontological approaches regarding the origins of problems: behaviorism, which conceptualizes problems as being learned purely from environmental factors; and cognitive theory, which asserts that problems arise from the human tendency to think irrationally. Because of their drastically divergent conceptualizations of how problems arise, each theory targets drastically different change strategies (teaching new behaviors versus teaching better ways of thinking). Yet, cognitive behavioral theorists and therapists have been able to reconcile these two drastically different ideas about the origins of human problems and the counselor's role in helping people with problems into one coherent theory that allows counselors to work with both behaviors *and* thoughts.

While the theories of behaviorism and cognitive therapy might target different areas of change, they are not opposite from one another, like psychoanalysis and person-centered therapy. Psychoanalysis essentially views people as inherently bad and driven largely by unconscious drives, while person-centered theory views people as essentially good and driven by a conscious striving for self-actualization. These two views of human nature and the purpose of therapy are so different that it seems impossible to integrate them in any meaningful way.

There are certainly stark differences between the views of human nature espoused by psychoanalysis and those espoused by person-centered therapy and a potential conflict arises when these fundamental differences are viewed as mutually exclusive. According to Norcross, however, integrating such diverse views of human nature together is precisely what makes integration "interesting" because it allows practitioners to harness the individual strengths of diverse, but potentially complementary orientations (p. 17). Rather than asserting one fundamental view of human nature (i.e., people are inherently good or bad), theoretical integration allows practitioners to recognize both sides of human nature: people have, within them, both inherent good and evil. Similarly, an approach that integrates aspects of psychoanalysis and the person-centered approach can allow supervisors to facilitate supervisee growth by providing optimal conditions for self-actualization, while, at the same time, recognizing that supervisees can be stifled from growth because of unconscious defense mechanisms. Safran and Messer (1997) viewed this type of dialectical thinking that is inherent in meta-theoretical orientations as a tool that "allows one to take into account the paradoxes and contradictions that are inherent in life" (p. 145). These authors have also stated, "Rival systems are increasingly viewed not as adversaries, but as a welcome diversity; not as contradictory, but as complimentary" (p. 18).

It is important to note that this is not the first approach seeking to integrate salient aspects of psychodynamic theory with person-centered theory. In fact, Garfield and Kurtz (1977), in a survey that was conducted with practitioners over thirty years ago, found that psychodynamic/person-centered integration was the third most frequently reported theoretical combination among practitioners who identified as integrative.

As a narrative therapist, I agree with many of the theoretical principles you have outlined; however, I find it difficult to accept your use of Freud's theory, particularly your assertion about the role of the unconscious in protecting supervisees from experiencing potentially uncomfortable situations in therapy and supervision. Couldn't you reframe this more simply as supervisees being consciously resistant or cautious to change, rather than evoking Freud and subconscious processes?

I too was initially hesitant to integrate Freudian principles regarding the unconscious into this constructivist approach to understanding supervisee resistance. Like many counselors of my era, my graduate training in psychoanalysis was positioned more as a "history of the field" than a detailed instruction in the practice of psychoanalysis. Additionally, much of my early learning experiences focused on recognizing the limitations of psychoanalysis from a multicultural, feminist, and postmodern perspective rather than understanding the contributions of Freud to the field. I am certainly aware, therefore, of the salient limitations inherent in conceptualizing clinical supervision through a Freudian lens. I also recognize that not all forms of resistance occur at an unconscious level; supervisees can be fully conscious of their resistances toward certain forms of growth, but still remain unable to overcome these resistances without the assistance of the supervisor.

However, much of the resistance I have noticed supervisees experience in supervision does not appear to derive from consciousness awareness. I base this assertion on two observations. First, supervisees often will state that they never heard or noticed client behaviors or statements that they later find to be strongly connected to the dynamics of change which they seek to resist (see Chapter 2 for examples). Second, supervisees often express extreme surprise and bewilderment at their realizations regarding their unconscious resistances, often saying things like, "how could I have not realized something so obvious?" These two factors, which I have seen repeated numerous times during supervision, have led me to conclude that they were not consciously aware of their resistances.

Given my recognition of the role of the unconscious in providing resistances to supervisee change and growth, it is difficult for me to frame this phenomenon using any other theoretical approach. Although my constructive approach for dealing with unconscious defenses in supervision is drastically different from many forms of psychoanalysis, I remain appreciative of Freud's groundbreaking work in discovering and illuminating the role of the unconscious in human problems. I am inclined, therefore, to agree with the conclusion of noted existential therapist Irving Yalom (2002), who succinctly stated, "Freud was not always wrong" (p. 217).

You noted in Chapter 1 that theories of counselor development are an important part of this approach; yet, you only provided a very brief review of two of the theories of counselor development. Why didn't you include more details about this important aspect of the constructive approach?

Indeed, theories of counselor development are central in helping both supervisors and supervisees understand and normalize their experiences in supervision. My assumption is that many readers are already familiar with most of the theories I have outlined in this book, including theories of counselor development. Therefore, in the interest of space, I decided to provide only brief reviews of all the theories I have integrated to form this constructive approach and to focus my reviews on the applied aspects of each theory. Readers who are unfamiliar with the models of counselor development that I have referenced in Chapter 1, or any of the other theories referred to in this book, are encouraged to read the primary sources from which I have drawn these brief reviews. In addition to providing more context regarding the ways in which I have integrated and applied the various theories, the original sources may also provide readers with alternative (and perhaps better!) ways of conceptualizing how these theories can be understood and applied to the context of clinical supervision.

While you articulated how theories of counselor development can be used to understand and normalize the experiences of supervisees at various developmental levels, you failed to articulate how these developmental theories have already been applied to clinical supervision. In fact, this constructive approach actually seems at odds with some of the things we know about developmental clinical supervision, including the fact that beginning supervisees need more teaching and structure.

Yes, I have chosen not to integrate some aspects of the developmental approaches to clinical supervision that I believe to be incompatible with constructivist ideas of change and growth. One noteworthy conflict, as you point out, involves how supervisors address the high levels of anxiety and low levels of professional knowledge that are associated with early stages of counselor development. Some developmental models, such as the Integrated Developmental Model (IDM; Stoltenberg, 1997), suggest that supervisors should be more directive, didactic, and structured with supervisees who are in the beginning developmental stages and provide regular reassurance to ease anxiety. It is only in later stages, when supervisees are more knowledgeable and less anxious, according to the IDM, that supervisors can begin to implement a more consultative role.

This assertion regarding the need to heavily structure early clinical experiences is counter to the propositions outlined in the developmental–constructivist theories described in Chapter 1 regarding the role of anxiety, ambiguity, and disequilibrium in human change processes. As I have outlined throughout this book, rather than seeking to minimize anxiety through use of teaching and scaffolding, constructive supervisors strive to help supervisees become comfortable with anxiety and disequilibrium in order to facilitate supervisee growth and development.

Like many other supervisors, I was originally trained to use a developmental approach to supervision that encouraged me to be much more didactic with new trainees; however, I eventually found this approach limited supervisee reflectivity and led some to become dependent upon me for answers. So, I began experimenting with the more reflective, consultative approach that I have outlined in this book. Surprisingly, my supervisees located in the beginning stages of counselor development quickly rose to the challenge of finding their own answers, even those who had just started their professional training and lacked the professional skills, experience, and self-efficacy that are normally considered prerequisites to using the consultant role in supervision. Through continued practice, I developed more and better ways of helping supervisees in beginning stages of development engage in the process of critical self-reflection by implementing the consultant role. Through my own process of critical self-reflection over the past fifteen years, I now feel comfortable in challenging the long-held assumption that all supervisees in early developmental stages need heavily structured, scaffolded, didactic approaches to succeed in supervision. Rather, my contention is that all counselors have the potential to develop their own answers and to develop skills of critical self-reflection, when provided with the right supervisory conditions.

Interestingly, while there have been studies that support the assertion that beginning supervisees need more structure and teaching than more advanced supervisees, Ladany, Marotta, and Muse-Burke (2001) argued that many of these studies lacked methodological rigor, particularly in the ways in which they operationalized supervisee developmental level, and that they focused only on supervisor perspectives of what they believed supervisees needed rather than assessing the actual needs of supervisees. Using a complex definition of supervisee developmental level, Ladany et al. conducted a study of one hundred counselor education students to assess, among other things, if supervisees preferred differing approaches based on their developmental level. Results indicated that supervisee developmental level did not predict their preference for supervisee style and that beginning supervisees did not prefer a more structured or didactic approach. The authors concluded, "the theoretical assumption that beginning trainees need more structure is an overgeneralization or a misguided view based more on clinical lore than on research" (p. 215).

It is important to note that I am not asserting that supervisors abandon their developmental approaches in working with beginning trainees. I am simply providing an alternative lens through which to view the developmental needs of supervisees from a constructivist perspective and the tools with which to facilitate supervisee growth from this alternative lens.

While you provided a rationale for and description of how the constructive approach can be used to facilitate multicultural competence in supervision, you failed to describe how supervisors operating from a constructive approach can encourage supervisees to become change agents and advocates for clients from marginalized groups.

This point leads to a central tension that exists within the constructivist paradigm. While all constructivists share a belief that the self is socially constituted, existing only in relationship to and with others, differences exist between constructivist counselors regarding the role of personal agency and locus of control in change processes. *Social* constructivists assert that the self has limited agency because of external social power structures. In other words, despite an individual's wish to change and grow, she may be unable to because of societal forces that marginalize and discriminate against her. As a result, counselors and supervisors operating from a social constructivist paradigm often focus their interventions on client advocacy and on bringing about societal change to reduce or remove barriers that have created or contributed to client problems.

A second group of constructivists, sometimes referred to as *personal* constructivists, focus more on client or supervisee individual agency within social structures. While personal constructivists do not deny the obstacles to personal change that are created by oppressive societal structures, they seek to deeply understand individual perceptions about these oppressive structures without imposing their own views on how clients can best address these issues. This does not mean that personal constructivists refrain from advocacy or systemic change; on the contrary, they are often deeply involved in systemic change efforts. However, advocacy and systems change become a focus of their counseling or supervision interventions when clients or supervisees introduce them.

Consistent with Mahoney's constructive approach to psychotherapy, the constructive approach to supervision articulated in this book is rooted in more of a personal constructivist approach, which discourages supervisors from prioritizing one form of helping over another. Rather, by consistently raising questions that help supervisees think critically about potential injustices in their clients' lives, constructive supervisors assist supervisees in identifying their own understandings of the problem and in deciding for themselves on the proper target of change, which can be at the individual and/or systemic level.

As stated previously, this book represents merely one attempt to connect constructivist ideas to the practice of clinical supervision. Readers should make their own interpretations about how constructivist ideas can be applied to their supervision practice in ways that are consistent with their own values regarding effective multicultural supervision. Supervisors who identify strongly with social constructivist views of multicultural counseling and supervision can and should apply these same advocacy-based principles in supervision, as long as their stances are clearly articulated to their supervisees.

You mentioned in Chapter 3 that you prefer to review tapes with supervisees; however, isn't it true that taping can greatly increase supervisee anxiety to the point that it can impair their abilities to assist their clients?

In my experience, most supervisees, even seasoned counselors who have prior experiences with taping, are initially anxious about taping their counseling sessions and reviewing these tapes with a new supervisor. This anxiety can manifest in many ways, from directly refusing to tape, to more subtle delays that impede the presentation of tapes (e.g., failing to get clients' permissions, technological glitches). As I have articulated throughout this book, the core of the constructive approach is not to reduce supervisee anxiety, but to help them embrace their anxiety as a necessary ingredient to learning, growth, and development. Constructive supervisors, therefore, have a number of tools available to them to help supervisees work through anxiety they may experience regarding taping, which includes establishing a caring, empathic, non-judgmental relationship with them; conveying an acceptance of multiple right ways of conducting counseling; and teaching supervisees to embrace mindfulness-based principles. In fact, anxiety around taping issues can often serve as an excellent way of introducing constructivist and mindfulness-based principles about anxiety since taping is often discussed early in the supervision experience.

Interestingly, while I believe that taping often contributes to supervisee anxiety, research does not support the assertion. In fact, Ellis, Krengel, and Beck (2002) found that taping not only failed to increase the anxiety of supervisees, but also did not have any negative effect on the experiences of clients, even for neophyte counselors. The benefits of taping in terms of providing an opportunity to critically reflect upon their sessions, therefore, greatly outweigh any potential harm that might occur to supervisees or clients as a result of their anxiety about the issue.

Has there been any research to support the efficacy of the constructive approach?

The constructive approach integrates theory and technique from several empirically supported approaches to education, psychotherapy, and clinical supervision.

As described in Chapter 2, numerous studies support the importance of the supervisor/supervisee relationship as conceptualized in this approach, and decades of research highlight the benefits fostering intrinsic motivation as articulated in Self-Determination Theory. Additionally, a growing body of research supports the use of mindfulness in a wide range of psychotherapeutic and counselor education contexts. There has even been research to support the need to examine the role of unconscious forces in counseling and supervision (Ladany, Constantine, Miller, & Erickson, & Muse-Burke, 2000). The approach, therefore, is based upon a solid foundation of empirically supported approaches.

Although the constructive approach is relatively new, there has been one study, conducted by Alisa Hathaway (2012), that specifically examined constructive supervision. Upon learning about and using constructive supervision in my doctoral supervision class, Alisa was interested in exploring the experiences of supervisors and supervisees who were using the constructive approach in clinical mental health settings. Alisa recruited two former doctoral students from our program who strongly identified as constructive supervisors and who supervised in different mental health settings (adult and child populations) to participate in the study. For her research, Alisa taped and analyzed several of their supervision sessions and conducted interviews with both supervisors and their supervisees to explore their perceptions of supervising from, and being supervised by, the constructive approach. Using an interpretive inquiry method of qualitative research, Alisa analyzed data from the sessions and interviews and developed several descriptive themes regarding how these mental health supervisors and their supervisees experienced constructive supervision.

The first theme that arose was that all participants felt the approach facilitated a strong supervisor/supervisee relationship. Specifically, a strong relationship was facilitated when supervisors: (a) expressed unconditional acceptance of their supervisees, including accepting their limitations; (b) were fully present with supervisees during sessions; and (c) demonstrated trust in supervisees to find their own answers. A second theme was the importance of the supervisor having a solid understanding of the developmental level of the supervisee, which allowed the supervisor to understand and empathize with supervisee developmental struggles and to normalize aspects of this development. Third, both supervisees and supervisors described the benefits of facilitating supervisee critical self-reflection in ways consistent with the constructive approach. Self-reflection was perceived as most powerfully facilitated when supervisors adhered strongly to the inquirer role, which included providing reflective questions and activities; used metaphor and metaphoric activities; and refrained from providing direct advice or compliments of their work. A fourth theme that emerged was a mutual recognition regarding the powerful role of the unconscious in evoking supervisee resistances to change. Both supervisors and supervisees asserted that a strong supervisor/supervisee relationship, an openness on the part of the supervisor to explore this area, and modeling on the part of the supervisor to explore his or her own unconscious resistance assisted supervisees in skillfully reflecting upon this difficult aspect of self-awareness.

Additionally, all participants perceived the approach as effective in community mental health settings, although both supervisors acknowledged the need to occasionally deviate from a purely reflective/consultative role in order to directly address administrative matters such as supervisee productivity, documentation, and crisis/safety issues. However, they also stated the ease and comfort with which they were able to become more directive once the core conditions of the constructive approach had been firmly established. Additionally, the supervisors described strategies they had developed that allowed them to be more directive in ways that did not impede the egalitarian process inherent in the constructive approach. For example, one supervisor described integrating the narrative technique of "externalizing the problem" (p. 120) as an effective means of weaving a more directive supervisory stance into the constructive model. Rather than the supervisee feeling as if she was the problem, this externalizing of the issue, according to this supervisor, allowed them to mutually own and navigate the problem together.

While more research is needed to better understand the conditions under which constructive supervision can be most effective, the findings suggest utility of the model in a wide range of professional settings, including clinical mental health settings.

I would like to integrate more of a constructive approach but I'm concerned that supervisees who are used to a more traditional style of supervision will misinterpret my trying to pull answers from them as me being lazy or incompetent. Do you have any suggestions for helping supervisees understand the importance of developing their own answers in supervision?

Yes, in addition to clearly explaining my approach and my rationale for implementing the approach, I also sometimes share a story with supervisees that can assist in illustrating this fundamental aspect of the constructive approach. I became aware of this story several years ago from a supervisor-in-training who was informed of the story by her supervisee. As a narrative therapist, this supervisor had developed a practice of occasionally sharing a small gift with her clients at the conclusion of therapy to symbolically represent a meaningful aspect of the client's progress in therapy or the counselor/client relationship. This supervisor was someone for whom the constructive approach resonated strongly and she was quickly able to adapt and implement it in her work with her supervisee.

During their final supervision session together, the supervisor gave her supervisee two butterfly charms and told her that one was meant to represent her, as a counselor, and the other one represented her future clients. The supervisor did not share her understanding of the meaning of these charms with her and, instead, asked her supervisee to construct her own meaning behind the metaphoric offering. A few months later, the supervisee sent the supervisor an email indicating that she had finally found the meaning of the charms she had received from her supervisor. The supervisee said she had always kept her butterfly charms with her while conducting therapy, but had not understood their meaning until reading the following story:

WHY THE BUTTERFLY DIED

There once was a little boy in India who walked up to a Guru Indian Wise Man, who was sitting looking at something in his hand. The little boy went up to look at it and asked the Guru "What is that?"

"It's a cocoon," the Guru tells him. "Inside the cocoon is a butterfly. Soon the cocoon is going to split and the butterfly will come out."

"Could I have it?" asks the little boy.

"Yes," says the Guru, "but you must promise me that, when the cocoon splits and the butterfly starts to come out and he is beating his wings to get out of the cocoon, you won't help him. Don't help the butterfly by breaking his cocoon apart. Let him do it by himself."

The little boy promised, took the cocoon, went home with it, and then sat and watched. Finally, the cocoon split. Inside was a beautiful, damp butterfly, frantically beating its wings against the cocoon, trying to get out and not being able to do it. The little boy desperately wanted to help. Finally he gave in and disobeyed the Guru's orders. He pushed the two halves of the cocoon apart and the butterfly sprang out. But, as soon as it got up into the air, it fell down to the ground and was killed. The little boy picked up the dead butterfly and in tears went back to the Guru and showed it to him.

"You see, little boy," the Guru said, "you pushed open the cocoon, didn't you?"

"Yes, said the little boy, "I did."

And the Guru said, "You don't understand. You didn't see what you were doing. When the butterfly comes out of the cocoon, the only way he can strengthen his wings is by beating them against the cocoon. It beats against the cocoon so its muscles will grow. When you helped it the way you did, you prevented it from getting strong. That's why the butterfly fell to the ground and died."

As a new therapist, the supervisee described how painful it had been for her to see her clients struggling so intensively with their issues and how helpless she felt in not being able to do more to ease their struggles. The story, she said, helped her recognize that client struggles are a necessary component of their healing process. As a result of this awareness, she felt more comfortable being fully present with clients as they processed and experienced their intense struggles. Likewise, she also recalled times that her supervisor had patiently and empathically allowed her to struggle to find her own answers during supervision. She now recognized that her supervisor's patience in allowing her to struggle and find her own answers in supervision had ultimately made her a stronger and more competent therapist.

To me, this story beautifully captures the essence of the constructive approach. The idea of allowing supervisees to struggle does not always feel like the most compassionate or expedient way of helping them grow as counselors, especially when it feels so much easier to simply give them the answers they are struggling to find. Yet, as the story points out, it is only through engaging in these struggles that supervisees develop the strength and resources to successfully engage in their own practice. The story was so moving to me that I now frequently share it with supervisees and students so that they can better understand my philosophy of supervision/teaching and so they can better conceptualize the struggles of their future clients. Of course, supervisees have occasionally pointed out to me that the guru probably could have prevented the death of the butterfly had he simply provide the rationale for not helping the butterfly (recall from Chapter 3 that providing a rationale for advice is central to the constructive approach). While I agree with this suggestion in principle, the story would not be as impactful had the guru fully explained his rationale ahead of time. Additionally, the learning might also not have been as impactful for the boy in the story had he not had the experience of actively seeing and feeling the results of his actions. The story, therefore, also highlights the power of experiential learning and the need to have someone with whom to process reflections of the learning experiences.

Unfortunately, I have not been able to identify an author of this story. The first reference to the story that I found comes from an audio recording by a motivational speaker named Earl Nightingale who hosted a weekly radio show in the 1950s. Nightingale shared the poem in his radio address and attributed it to Henry Miller, an American writer most famous for his 1934 classic, *The Tropic of Cancer*; however, I was unable to find this story in any of Miller's work. This process of attempting to track down the author of the story led me to another of Miller's (1951) quotes that I also share with supervisees who are struggling to find their own answers. The following quote is particularly useful to share with supervisees who express frustration with supervisors who fail to provide them direct answers when they ask for them:

> No [person] is great enough or wise enough for any of us to surrender our destiny to. The only way in which anyone can lead us is to restore to us the belief in our own guidance.

Faith in one's self is not created simply through receiving praise from supervisors or through direct instruction. This quote from Miller provides another opportunity for constructive supervisors to explain their rationale for allowing supervisees to struggle in finding their own answers. As illustrated in the butterfly story, it can be difficult to watch supervisees struggle to break free of the shells that have bound them. However, supervisors can demonstrate a deep faith in supervisees through incorporating a self-reflective approach in which supervisors patiently and empathically join with supervisees in helping them discover their own answers.

References

Asay, T.P., & Lambert, M.J. (1999). The empirical case for the common factors in therapy: Quantitative findings. In M.A. Hubble, B.L. Duncan & S.D. Miller (Eds.), *The heart and soul of change: What works in therapy* (pp. 23–55). Washington, DC: American Psychological Association.

Crocket, K. (2004). Storying counselors: Producing professional selves in supervision. In D.A. Paré, & G. Larner (Eds.), *Collaborative practice in psychology and therapy* (pp. 171–182). New York: Haworth Press.

Ellis, M.V., Krengel, M., & Beck, M. (2002). Testing self-focused attention theory in clinical supervision: Effects of supervisee anxiety and performance. *Journal of Counseling Psychology, 49*(1), 101.

Garfield, S.L., & Kurtz, R. (1977). A study of eclectic views. *Journal of Consulting and Clinical Psychology, 45*(1), 78–83.

Guiffrida, D.A. (2006). Toward a cultural advancement of Tinto's theory. *The Review of Higher Education, 29*(4), 451–472.

Guiffrida, D.A. (2009). Theories of human development that enhance our understanding of the college transition process. *Teachers College Record, 111*(10), 2419–2443.

Guiffrida, D.A., & Douthit, K.Z. (2010). The African American college student experience at predominantly white institutions: Implications for school and college counselors. *Journal of Counseling & Development, 88*(3), 311–318.

Hathaway, A.P. (2012). *Experiences of supervisors and supervisees utilizing a constructivist approach to supervision in community mental health settings* (Doctoral dissertation, University of Rochester. Margaret Warner Graduate School of Education and Human Development).

Jensen, J.P., Bergin, A.E., & Greaves, D.W. (1990). The meaning of eclecticism: New survey and analysis of components. *Professional Psychology: Research and Practice, 21*(2), 124–130.

King, D., & Wheeler, S. (2007). The responsibilities of counsellor supervisors: A qualitative study. *British Journal of Guidance and Counselling, 27*(2), 215–229.

Ladany, N., Marotta, S., & Muse-Burke, J. (2001). Supervisee integrative complexity, experience, and preference for supervisor style. *Counselor Education and Supervision, 40*, 203–219.

Ladany, N., Constantine, M.G., Miller, K., Erickson, C.D., & Muse-Burke, J.L. (2000). Supervisor countertransference: A qualitative investigation into its identification and description. *Journal of Counseling Psychology, 47*(1), 102.

Lambert, M.J., & Bergin, A.E. (1992). Achievements and limitations of psychotherapy research. In D.K. Freedhiem, H. Freudenberger & J.W. Kessler (Eds.), *History of psychotherapy: A century of change* (1st ed., pp. 360–390). Washington, DC: American Psychological Association.

Mahoney, M.J. (2006). *Constructive psychotherapy: Theory and practice.* New York: Guilford.

Miller, H. (1951) *The wisdom of the heart.* New York: New Directions Publishing.

Neimeyer, R.A. (2009). *Constructivist psychotherapy: Distinctive features.* New York: Routledge.

Norcross, J.C. (2005). A primer on psychotherapy integration. In J.C. Norcross, & M.R. Goldfried (Eds.), *Handbook of psychotherapy integration* (2nd ed., pp. 3–23). New York: Oxford University Press.

Orlinsky, D., Cierpka, M., Aapro, N., Buchheim, P., Bae, S., Davidson, C., et al. SPR Collaborative Res Network. (1999). Development of psychotherapists: Concepts, questions, and methods of a collaborative international study. *Psychotherapy Research, 9*(2), 127–153.

Rigazio-Digilio, S.A., Gonçalves, O.F., & Ivey, A.E. (1996). From cultural to existential diversity: The impossibility of psychotherapy integration within a traditional framework. *Applied and Preventive Psychology, 5*(4), 235–247.

Safran, J., & Messer, S. (1997). Psychotherapy integration: A postmodern critique. *Clinical Psychology-Science and Practice, 4*(2), 140–152.

Speedy, J. (2010). Consulting with gargoyles: Applying narrative ideas and practices in counselling supervision. *European Journal of Psychotherapy and Counselling, 3*(3) 419–431.

Stoltenberg, C.D. (1997). The integrated developmental model of supervision. *Psychotherapy in Private Practice, 16*(2), 59–69.

Tinto, V. (1993). *Leaving college: Rethinking the causes and cures of student attrition.* Chicago: University of Chicago Press.

Vincent, N. & LeBow, M. (1995). Treatment preference and acceptability: Epistemology and locus of control, *Journal of Constructivist Psychotherapy, 8*, 81–96.

Wampold, B.E. (2001). *The great psychotherapy debate: Models, methods, and findings.* New York: Routledge.

Watkins, C.E. (2011). Psychotherapy supervision since 1909: Some friendly observations about its first century. Journal of Contemporary Psychotherapy, *41*(2) 57–67.

Wheeler, S., & Richards, K. (2007). The impact of clinical supervision on counsellors and therapists, their practice and their clients: A systematic review of the literature. *Counselling and Psychotherapy, 7*(1), 54–65.

Winter, D.A. (1990). Therapeutic alternatives for psychological disorder. In G.J. Neimeyer and R.A. Neimeyer (Eds.), *Advances in Personal Construct Psychology, Vol. 1* (pp. 89–116). Greenwich, CT: JAI.

Yalom, I. (2002). *The gift of therapy: An open letter to a new generation of therapists and their patients.* New York: Harper Collins.

APPENDIX

Constructive Supervisee Assessment (CSA)

Key:
Has not yet demonstrated this skill 1
Rarely demonstrates this skill   2
Has begun demonstrating this skill 3
Skillfully demonstrates this skill   4

The supervisee

Is creative during counseling sessions	1	2	3	4
Is able to adapt approaches during sessions when confronted with challenges or surprises	1	2	3	4
Occasionally takes risks and moves outside of her or his comfort zone	1	2	3	4
Is sensitive to the cultural needs of clients	1	2	3	4
Arrives at supervision with meaningful questions to discuss	1	2	3	4
Presents areas in supervision in which he or she is struggling	1	2	3	4
Is patient with her or himself in identifying areas in need of improvement	1	2	3	4
Strives to use descriptive, non-judgmental language when attending to areas in need of improvement	1	2	3	4
Is able to identify perceived strengths and capitalize on them	1	2	3	4
Is able to identify areas in which growth has occurred	1	2	3	4
Is able to conceptualize client issues using established theoretical orientations	1	2	3	4

Is able to utilize personal constructs and experiences in conceptualizing client issues	1	2	3	4
Can critically evaluate his or her chosen orientation(s)	1	2	3	4
Understands that there are multiple ways to conduct counseling	1	2	3	4
Actively engages in the process of constructing her or his own answers when questions arise	1	2	3	4
Consults counseling literature and colleagues to find answers	1	2	3	4
Seeks to understand how his or her own cultural biases are affecting work with clients	1	2	3	4
Is curious to explore how personal issues may be affecting her or his conceptualizations of client issues	1	2	3	4
Is open to exploring how personal defenses can impact work with clients	1	2	3	4
Is open to exploring how personal defenses can become impediments to making meaningful changes during supervision	1	2	3	4
Openly, yet critically evaluates suggestions and alternatives provided by the supervisor	1	2	3	4

Comments:

New learning that resulted from the supervision/evaluation process:

Plans for implementing new learning:

* Use of the CSA is free and does not require permission of the author. Researchers using the CSA are asked to cite the complete reference information.

INDEX

Abel, D. 46
acceptance and commitment therapy 31
Adler, A. 3
advice 9–12, 14–16, 25–9, 50–7, 71–75,
    107–09, 121
agency 107–09, 131
agents 3; travel 25
Allen, N.B. 34
amotivation 28–9
Amundson, N.E. 77–9
Andrews, J. 97
anxiety 4, 7, 11–14, 17, 29–34, 65–9, 99,
    129–30, 132
archeology of therapy activity 107–09
Argyris, C. 13
Asay, T.P. 126
assessment, activities 104–09; challenges
    of 111–15; constructivist principles of
    100–02; process of 102–04
Atkinson, D.R. 68
autonomy-supportive environment
    28–30, 44
Aveline, M. 141

Bachler, E. 34
Bae, S. 138
Baird, F. 97
balance 6, 49–50, 82
Bandura, A. 3, 17
Barkham, M. 141

Barnes, K.L. 77, 104
Bateson, G. 3
Beck, K.L. 132
Bergin, A.E. 127
Bernard, J.L. ix–xvii, 10, 19, 21, 23,
    41–2, 45, 48–50, 58, 61–2, 68, 70,
    73–4, 75, 79, 97, 99, 104, 112,
    115, 141
Blackmon, B. 70
Bond, F.W. 31
Borders, L.D. 70
Brown, A.P. 35
Bruner, J. 3
Buddha see Buddhism
Buddhism 3, 31–2, 93
bug-in-the-ear approach 59
Bugental, J. 3
butterfly story 135–7

Cade, R. 97
Campbell, J. 13
Carlsen, M.B. 54
Cashwell, C.S. 61–2, 73
Cavalieri, C.E. 71, 73
Chambers, R. 34, 45
Change 4–8, 13–14, 26–8; 38–9, 65–9,
    agents of 126–7
Chirkov, V. 28, 45
Christopher, J.C. 45, 65, 90, 97–8
Cierpka, M. 138

Clark, D.J. 97
client facetime activity 88–90
Cochran, B.N. 31, 46
Coker, J.K. 82, 98
competence, demonstrating 16–7; motivation 27–35
Consoli, A.J. 73
Constantine, M.G. 133, 137
constructive supervisee assessment (CSA) 111
constructivism, introduction to 1–4; model of change 4–8,; model of counselor education *see* also "emergence model"; model of counselor development 8–13
Corey, G. 104, 116
countertransference 39, 43–44, 58
Crocket, K. 5, 19, 119, 137
Cueva, C. 97–8

D'Andrea, M. 67, 70, 73
D'Iuso, N. 99, 115
Davidson, C. 138
Deci, E.L. xiv, xvi, 21, 25–8, 45–7
defense mechanisms 7, 38–45, 58, 128
denial 39–41, 58
Dewey, J. 86, 97
dialectical behavioral therapy 31
Diehl, N.S. 88, 98
discrimination model 49–51; consultant role 51–4; counselor role 57–8; teacher role 52–7
Douthit, K.Z. 124, 137
Dowling, S. 104, 115
Dressel, J.L. 68, 73
Duan, C. 69, 73
Dulko, J.P. 71, 73

Efran, J.S. 73
Ellis, M.V. 99, 115, 132, 137
emergence model 13–18, 62–6
empathy 23–2, 35, 94–5
epigenetic principle 5
Epston, D. 84, 98, 107, 108, 115
Eriksen, C.D. 133, 137
Eriksen, K. xiv, xvi, 1, 13, 20
Erikson, E.H. 5, 19
evaluation *see* assessment
existential 2, 124
experiments 39, 53–6, 77
extrinsic motivation 27–8

Fauber, R.L. 55, 73
feedback mechanism 7–8
feedback, giving 11, 58–9, 110–15
feedforward mechanism 7–8
Felice, A.D. 71, 73
Fletcher, K. 32, 46
Fong, M.L. 59, 73
Francis, D. 86, 88, 97
Frankel, Z.E. 38, 46
Frankl, V. 3
Freeman, E.M. 19, 70, 74
Freitas, G.F. 99, 116
Freud, S. xiv, xvi, 26, 38, 41, 43, 46, 128, 129

gatekeeping 22, 117–20
Gatmon, D. 69, 73
Goncalves, O.F. 4, 19, 67, 74, 127
Goodyear, R.K. xi, xii, xiii, xvi, 10, 15, 19, 21, 26, 41, 42, 45, 46, 50, 58, 62, 68, 70, 73, 75, 97, 99, 104, 112, 115
Greaves, D.W. 127, 137
Grepmair, L. 34, 36, 90, 97
Grossman, P. 94, 97
Guidano, V.F. 3, 102, 116
Guiffrida, D.A. i, iii, iv, ix, x, xiv, xvi, 13, 14, 19, 29, 35, 45, 46, 59, 62, 73, 77, 78, 79, 81, 97, 98, 124, 137
Gullone, E. 34, 45

Hackney, H. 15, 19, 26, 46
Hall, P.D. 34, 46
Hansen, J. 67, 73
Hart, T. 4, 34, 46
Hathaway, A.P. 133, 137
Hayes, S.C. 31, 46
Haynes, R. 104, 116
Heraclitus 3
Hill, C.E. 99, 116
Hinton, D.E. 94, 97
Hird, J.S. 71, 73
Ho, T.A. 91
Hoffman, M.A. 99, 116
Hoffman, R. 85, 98
Hofmann, S.G. 94
Holmes, S.E. 99, 116

inquirer role 60–1, 133
Integrated Developmental Model 10, 130
interpersonal process recall 60–2

intrinsic motivation 27–30, 49, 62, 110, 124, 133
Ishiyama, F.I. 78, 98
Ivey, A.E. 4, 19, 67, 74, 127, 138

Jackson, D. 19, 73
James, W. 3
Jensen, J.P. 127, 137
Jones, W.P. 82, 98
Jordan, R.A. 77, 97

Kabat-Zinn, J. xiv, xvi, 32, 35, 46, 91, 94, 98
Kadushin, A. 104, 116
Kagan, N.I. 60, 61, 74
Kagan, H. 60, 61, 74
Kant, I. 73, 74
Kaplan, U. 28, 45
Karasu, T.B. 66, 74
Kegan, R. 8, 19
Kehrer, C.A. 31, 46
Kelly, G.A. 3, 4, 19, 105
Kim, B.S. 28, 68, 73
Kim, Y. 45
King, D. 118
Kirschenbaum, H. xvii, 22, 74
knowing: dialectical 9–10; received/ conventional 8–9; self-authorized 9–10
knowledge 1–3, 12–18, 25, 50, 63–7, 100–03, 108, 118–21
known information questions 52–54
Kohlberg, L. 8, 19
Korzybski, A. 105, 116
Koshkarian, L. 73
Krathwohl, D.R. 61, 74
Krengel, M. 132, 137, 143
Kress, V.E. 85, 98
Krishnamurti, J. 13, 19
Kurtz, R. 128, 137

Ladany, N. 99, 115–16, 130, 133, 137
Lambert, M.J. 126, 137
Lao Tzu 3
Larner, G. 19, 137
Leary, T. 2
LeBow, M. 122, 138
Lehrman-Waterman, D. 99, 102, 116
Leong, F.T. 72, 74
Levitt, H.M. 38, 46
lifespan theory of counselor development 10–13

Lillis, J. 31, 46
Linehan, M.M. 31, 46
live supervision 58–9
Logan, S.L. 70, 74
Lovell, C.W. 9–10, 20
Luke, M. 50, 74
Luoma, J.B. 31, 46
Lyddon, W.J. 1–3, 19
Lynch, M. xvii, 26, 29, 46–7

Mahoney, M.J. xii–xvii, 19–26, 20, 22, 25, 38, 46, 73–4, 76, 88, 98, 115–16, 126, 131, 137
Maris, J.A. 34–5, 45, 90, 97
Markos, P.A. 82–3, 98
Marotta, S. 130, 137
Marquis, A. xxvii, 35, 45, 126
Martso-Perry, N. 73
Masuda, A. 31, 46
McAuliffe, G.J. xiv, xvi, 1, 8–10, 13, 20
McNeill, B.W. xvi, 20
McRoy, R.G. 70, 74
meditation, mindful breathing 91–3; lovingkindness/compassion 93–5;
Mehan, H. 53, 74
metaphoric drawing activities 77–82
Mezirow, J. 13, 20
Miller, H. 136–7
Miller, J. 13, 20, 32, 46
Miller, K. 133, 137
Miller, S.D. 137
mindful eating activity 96
mindfulness 31–8, 123–5; activities; see also meditation; research about 34–5
mirror time activity 88–9
mistakes 11–13, 17, 24, 119–20,
Mitterlehner, F. 34, 46
modeling 14, 17,
Modernism 1–4,
Molinaro, M. 99, 116
Moreno, J.L. 105–116
Morgan, M.M. 34, 47, 90, 98
motivation see intrinsic and extrinsic motivation
Moulton, P. 104, 116
multicultural, competence 131–2; learning objectives 66–72
Murakami, Y. 96, 98
Muse-Burke, J.L. 130, 133, 137

narrative, therapy 84–5, 118–19, 128, 134
Neimeyer, G.J. 14, 20, 100–01, 109
Neimeyer, R.A. xiii, xvi, xvii, 2–4, 20, 22, 46, 53, 65, 67, 73–4, 76, 98, 105–6, 116–6, 123, 137–8
Nelson, K.W. 97–8
Nelson, M.L. 59, 92
Neufeldt, S.A. 51, 59, 73–4, 87, 98, 110, 116
Nickel, M. 34, 46
non-directiveness 25–6
non-judgmental 32–3, 36, 49, 55, 68, 72, 88, 90–6, 103, 111, 125, 136
Norcross, J.C. 126–7, 137
Nylund, D. 84–98

objectivism 1–2
Oliver, M. 97–8
Orlinski, D. 127

Palm, A. 88, 97
parallel process 41–3
Paré, D.A. xvii, 19, 137
Patel, N. 73
Patterson, C.H. 26, 46
Pearson, L. 84, 98
pedagogy, adult theories of learning 13; behaviorist 36, 59–60 spiritual/transformative 13
Pels, L.C. 106, 116
Perry, W.G. 8, 20
Person Centered Therapy 22–6, 124, 126–9
Personal Construct Theory 3–4
Piaget, J. 8, 20
postmodernism 2–3, 67–72
praise 30–1, 57, 136
protecting clients 15–16, 118–20
psychoanalytic therapy 38–45

reality tunnels 2–3
reflection, in-action 17–18; on-action 18
reflective journal writing activity 86–8
relationship, supervisor/supervisee 3–4, 22–4, 30–1, 35–45, 60–68, 71–2, 133–4
resistance, working with 4, 7, 38–9, 133
Richards, K. 118, 138
Rigazio-Digilio, S.A. 67, 74, 127
Roehlke, H. 69, 73
Rogers, C.R. xiv, xvi, xvii, 15, 21, 22–6, 29, 35, 45–7, 49, 51, 60, 74

Ronnestad, M.H. xiv, xvi, 10–12, 20
Rothaupt, J.W. 34, 47, 90, 98
Rother, W. 34, 46, 90, 97
Russell-Chapin, L.A. 34, 47, 98
Ryan, R.M. xiv, xvi, xvii, 21, 26–30, 35, 45–7
Rybak, C.J. 47, 98

Saiz, S. 77–81, 97
sand tray activity 82–4
Schon, D.A. 13, 17–20
Schopenhauer, A. 2
Segal, Z.V. xiv, xvi, 31, 47
self-characterization sketch 105–6
self-determination theory 26–31, 124, 133
Shiraishi, S. 96, 98
Siegel, R. 47
sine-wave activity 106–7
Skinner, B.F. 26, 47
Skovholt, T.M. xiv, xvi, 10–12, 20
Speedy, J. 117–18, 120, 138
stage theory 5–7
Steenbarger, B.N. 4–5, 20, 106, 116
Stoltenberg, C.D. xiv, xvi, 10, 20, 130, 138
Stone, D. 28–8, 47, 789, 97–8,
Strosahl, K.D. 31, 46
Sugamura, G. 96. 98

Teasdale, J.D. xiv, 31, 47
teleological 25
teleonomic 25
theoretical integration 126–8
therapeutic letter writing activity 84–5
Thomas, A.M. 85, 98
Thomas, J. 84, 98
Tinto, V. 124, 137–8
travel agents 25

unconditional positive regard 22–5, 31, 35
unconscious 38–44, 125–133

Vansteenkiste, M. 26, 28, 47
Vico, G. 3
video tape review 58–62
Vincent, N. 122, 138
vipassana 68
von Glasersfeld, E. 2, 13, 20

Wagner, N.S. 72, 74
Wall, A. 56, 88
Watkins, C.E. 46, 74, 118, 138
Watson, J.B. 26, 47

Weil, R. 1, 2, 19
Wheeler, S. 118, 137–8
Where am I activity 79–82
White, M. 84–5, 97–8, 107–8, 115
White, R.W. 27, 47
Williams, A.M. 88–90, 98

Williams, J.M.G. xiv, xvi, 31, 47
Wilson, K.G. 59, 89
Wilson, R.A. 2, 20
Winter, D.A. 122, 138
Wolgast, B. 99, 116
Woodworth, R.S. 27, 47

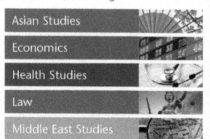